the song of roland

the song of roland   translated by
frederick bliss luquiens
introduction by nathan a. smyth
the macmillan company new york

contents

introduction

Before his death in 1940 Prof. Frederick B. Luquiens, a distinguished teacher of early French and other Romance languages at Yale University, completed but had never offered for publication a poetic translation of the Chanson de Roland. When the suggestion was made a few months ago that his classmates, of whom I was one, might want to publish it, I sent for the manuscript with the idea that a few hundred copies might be printed in pamphlet form for private distribution among his friends.

Like many another I had occasionally heard of the Song of Roland, and knew in a general way that it was a famous old French epic romanticizing a relatively unimportant incident in the withdrawal of Charlemagne's armies from Spain late in the eighth century; but I had never read or even seen a copy of it. The resultant impression had been that it was a sort of "museum piece" to be found only in the limbo of college and some larger libraries where it could be read by students and others especially interested in the early literature of France. So it was with a somewhat skeptical curiosity that I started to read the manuscript when it arrived.

That attitude soon changed to absorbed interest. I could not lay it down until it was read through to the end. "This is not a book for just a small group of friends," was the immediate reaction; "it should be published for wide distribution, to be read not only by students but by all lovers of romantic tales of the days when the chivalry of Christendom went forth to battle against the paynim Saracens."

Subsequent readings confirmed the belief that the Song of Roland, as here translated in melodious unrhymed pentameter, like that used by Tennyson in Idylls of the King, has seldom been surpassed or perhaps even equaled in interest, dramatic development and incidental lyric beauty by any narrative poetry that has come off the press in recent years.

What a skillful story-teller as well as master word painter and rare poet that old French troubadour was! Here in the Song of Roland, most famous of the Chansons de Geste in which were chanted fabulous tales of the glorious deeds of Charlemagne and his followers, we have a series of vivid pictures of successive events, each of which leads logically up to the next—the whole moving swiftly and inevitably to its dramatic conclusion with perfect continuity. With only a little adaptation, all of them would make colorful and absorbing cinematic scenes.

So graphic, however, are the written descriptions that it needs no camera to enable the reader to visualize them. Marsila, the Paynim King of Spain, for example, crouching "under the green boughs of olive trees" in "grim Saragossa, mountain-girt," and seeking counsel from his Moorish knights as to how to save himself from Charlemagne's fearful men; or the embassy of richly caparisoned Saracens bearing false promises, finding its way to where the "haughty Charles," snow-white of hair and beard, is seated on a throne of purest gold high in the Pyrenees, with Roland and his friend Oliver and many others around him playing chess and "games of fence"; and, later on, the Paynim hordes, pursuant to Marsila's plot with the Frankish traitor Ganelon, hiding among the grim defiles and in the black wood to ambush Charlemagne's rear guard in the Pass of Ronceval and there slaying all save Roland. And, finally, the unforgettable account, beggaring brief description, of how Roland came to his lonely and heroic death. Those and many others. Not anywhere in the narrative a word wasted, nor any spoken words not wed to action. Everywhere symmetry of form, coherence, unity.

There is romance also in the story of the development of the Roland legend and of its relationship and that of the Chanson to the historic events and rising passions which brought about the First Crusade, and of how through seven centuries the Chanson gradually sank into almost complete oblivion until, a little over a hundred years ago, it was suddenly brought forth into widespread and long continued renown.

Some hundred and fifty years before the event on which the legend is based Omar, the second of the Mohammedan Caliphs, captured Jerusalem and began to come into conflict with the Christians of the West. In 732 the Moslems, having overrun Spain and France as far as Poitiers were turned back by Charles Martel. During the next forty years a new dynasty, the Abbassides, arose among them and triumphed in the East over the Omayyads, who, however, retained control of Cordova and western Spain.

That was the developing situation when Charlemagne was recognized as King of all France in 771. During the next six years he was busy extending his domains, having started a war against the Saxons—which lasted for thirty-two years before they were conquered and Christianized—and gained control over almost all of Northern Italy. Then in 778 came his chance to move southward. The Abbasside governor of Barcelona formed a league against the Omayyad Emir of Cordova and, at his request, Charlemagne marched his army into Spain. The governor of Barcelona was to support him north of the river Ebro, where Charlemagne's sovereignty was to be recognized. In Murcia, to the southeast, the African Berbers were to aid them. But, after having taken Pamplona and started to lay siege to Saragossa on the Ebro, Charlemagne was called back to renewed fighting against the Saxons, and the siege was lifted.

The tragic event upon which the legend of Roland is based occurred as the French, on their way back, passed through the Basque province of Gascony in the lower Pyrenees. Little is known of the Basques in those days other than that, with the unquenchable zeal for independence which they have manifested down to our times, they were ready to fight against intrusion whether from Spaniard or from Frank.

The only authentic account of what took place is that found in the Life of Charlemagne written by his reputed secretary Eginhard. As translated by Prof. A. J. Grant * it reads:

Whilst the war with the Saxons was being prosecuted constantly and almost continuously he [Charlemagne] placed garrisons at suitable places on the frontier, and attacked Spain with the largest military expedition that he could collect. He crossed the Pyrenees, received the surrender of all the towns and fortresses that he attacked, and returned with his army safe and sound except for a reverse which he experienced through the treason of the Gascons on his return through the passes of the Pyrenees.

For while his army was marching in a long line, suiting their formation to the character of the ground and the defiles, the Gascons placed an ambuscade on the top of a mountain—where the density and extent of the woods in the neighborhood rendered it highly suitable for such a purpose—and then rushing down into the valley beneath threw into disorder the last part of the baggage train and also the rearguard which acted as a protection to those in advance.

In the battle which followed the Gascons slew their opponents to the last man. Then they seized upon the baggage, and under cover of the night, which was already falling, they scattered with the utmost speed. The Gascons were assisted in this feat by the lightness of their armor and the character of the ground where the affair took place. In this battle Eggihard, the surveyor of the royal table, Anselm,

* *Early Lives of Charlemagne*, by Eginhard and the Monk of Saint Gall (London, Chatto & Windus, 1922), pp. 19 ff.

the Count of the Palace, and Roland, Prefect of the Breton frontier, were killed along with many others. Nor could this assault be punished at once, for when the deed had been done the enemy so completely disappeared that they left behind them not so much as a rumor of their whereabouts.

From other sources, however, it has been learned that in the next year Charlemagne sent his son, Louis the Pious, back into Spain and, upon the fall of Barcelona a decade later, established the Spanish March (i.e., frontier military district) from the Pyrenees to the Ebro.

Here, so far as concerns this episode, history signs off; romance takes over.

Very soon, it would seem, tales of that gallant fight to the death began to spread from mouth to mouth. The jongleurs took it up and sang their cantilenas about it far and wide, even into adjacent lands. Ever the story grew and changed, more and more fabulous and romantic incidents being added. And so, for some three hundred years, songs of it were made and chanted in words and to music which have been forever lost, before there was written any version of it which has come down to us.

The question who wrote that first Chanson has been much discussed, but no certain answer has been found. Just when it was written is likewise uncertain—probably a few years before or after 1100. It too was lost. But a copy of it was made about fifty years later, only, in its turn, to disappear for some seven centuries before it finally came to light.

The three-hundred-odd years between the death of Roland and the birth of the written Song were characterized by events of great historic importance; events which gradually aroused the emotional reactions that are reflected in the legend as finally embodied in the Chanson and were themselves, it is believed, intensified by the singing of the Song throughout the domains of France.

In December 800, Charlemagne was crowned Emperor of the Holy Roman Empire. He succeeded in establishing friendly relations with the Mohammedans to such an extent that seven years later the famous Caliph Harun-al-Rashid acknowledged him as the Protector of Jerusalem and owner of the Church of the Sepulchre. Under his successors those relations deteriorated. In 1010 Caliph Hakim destroyed the Church and ended the protectorate. The capture of Jerusalem by the Seljukian Turks in 1071 made Christian access to that city so difficult that Western Christendom began to clamor for the conquest of the Holy Land.

The whole course of events had brought hatred of the Moslems to a white heat. Finally, in 1095 Pope Urban II preached the famous sermon which soon after resulted in the First Crusade.

The troubadours of those days not only were raconteurs and romanticizers of history but also, as they wandered hither and yon, were doubtless gatherers and purveyors of news. What they learned of current events could scarcely help influencing their songs. Pilgrimages to Rome were encouraged by the Church. Here and there along the routes were holy shrines where pilgrims tarried for their orisons. The minstrels who came to sing to them there would of course try to fashion their songs to the interests and emotions of their hearers. One such shrine was located at the Spanish village of Roncesvalles (Roncevaux in French) situated at an altitude of some 3,000 feet among the Pyrenees about five miles from the French frontier and near the valley known as Val Carlos where the battle is reputed to have been fought.

Under such influences it quite naturally came about that the treachery which destroyed the Franks was attributed to the hated Saracens instead of the Basques; also that the Chanson should develop into an epic of heroic battles fought and eventually won by Charlemagne's Christian knights against Marsila, king "of those who love not God and serve false gods of stone, brought from the shores of Araby."

Nor could the singing of that song, with its glorification of the mighty deeds of valor of the French knights of old, fail to arouse emulation among their descendants and eagerness to wreak vengeance upon and win final victory over the Mussulmans who for so many years had been trying to destroy Christianity.

Whether it was first written before or after 1095, it is clear, as is pointed out in a well informed account of

the First Crusade in the *Encyclopædia Britannica*, that
the Chanson de Roland "already contains the idea of
the holy war against Islam. The idea of the crusade had
thus already ripened in French poetry, before Urban
preached his sermon."

After Jerusalem was entered by the Crusaders in
1099 the French apparently began to lose interest in
the Song of Roland as well as in the other *chansons de
geste*. Partly, perhaps, because the dynasty of the Ca-
pets had supplanted the Carolingians. Perhaps even more
from the trend described by Prof. Luquiens in his Introduction to his *Three Lays of Marie de France, Retold
in English Verse*,* as follows:

About the middle of the twelfth century French literature
was in a critical state, near unto death from utter lack of
wholesome nourishment. All the meat had long since been
extracted from the themes of national tradition; poets and
audiences alike were beginning to tire of tales of Charlemagne and of Roland and of their sons and grandsons and
great-grandsons and of their fathers and grandfathers and
great-grandfathers. . . . So some writer, or perhaps several
writers at the same time, acting on one of those mysterious
common impulses which often affect men's thoughts, conceived the idea of turning to Celtic tradition; and for over
a century Celtism ruled French writing.

After that came the Renaissance, when interest in
early French literature was submerged by enthusiasm for
Greek and Latin art. The Roland legend, however, was
related in some prose compositions written in the fif-
* New York, Henry Holt & Co., 1911.

teenth century and was by no means wholly forgotten. In other lands it spread far and wide.

In Germany, early in the twelfth century, the priest Konrad made a translation of the Song which was paraphrased by the poet du Stricker about a century later. In Bremen, where Charlemagne had established a bishopric, there stands in front of the Rathaus a limestone statue of Roland some 17 1/2 feet high which, according to Baedeker, was erected in 1404 on the site of an earlier figure in wood. Similar but less impressive statues were set up in other cities in northern Germany, all representing Roland "the nephew of Charlemagne" as a "symbol of municipal jurisdiction and the palladium of civic liberty." A recent visitor to Bremen reports that the legend there current is to the effect that so long as that statue stands Germany will be the great central power in Europe but when it falls Germany will disintegrate.

In Italy there were written some romances about "Orlando," as Roland was called. Charlemagne and Roland are mentioned in Dante's Paradiso (Canto xviii) and there are statues of Roland and Oliver on the doorway of the cathedral of Verona.

In England the story of Roland became well known. According to the English historian William of Malmesbury and the Anglo-Norman chronicler Robert Wace, both writing in the twelfth century, the famous bard and warrior Taillefer led the Norman forces into battle at Hastings singing of Charlemagne and Roland and their vassals who died at Roncevaux. Chaucer, it is said, somewhere referred to a traitor as a "very Gamelin." To some extent the Chanson was read in original French texts. The legend was also recounted in various fifteenth century metrical romances about Charlemagne such as Rowlande's Song. In Shakespeare's *Henry VI* the Duke of Alençon, in warning the French Dauphin of the strength of the English, said:

> Froissart, a countryman of ours, records
> England all Olivers and Rowlands bred
> During the time Edward the Third did reign.

That estimate of their reputations tallies with the statement in Bartlett's *Familiar Quotations* * that the phrase "A Roland for your Oliver" originated because "their exploits are rendered so ridiculously and equally extravagant by the old romancers, that from them arose the saying, to signify matching one incredible lie with another, giving tit for tat, as good as one receives." An origin of the phrase more in tune with the spirit of ancient chivalry is given by Burton Stevenson † to the effect that "Roland and Oliver were two of Charlemagne's Paladins, so evenly matched, so legend says, that they fought for five days on an island in the Rhine, without either gaining the slightest advantage." Hence "a blow for a blow," a "tit for a tat."

* 11th Ed. (Boston, Little, 1937), p. 946.
† *Home Book of Proverbs, Maxims, and Familiar Phrases* (New York, Macmillan, 1948), p. 2003.

At last, through a succession of somewhat fortuitous events, came the discovery of the text of the Chanson as we now know it.

Thomas Allen, an Oxford M.A. and a noted mathematician and student of history and antiquity, had been indefatigable during his later years in collecting scattered ancient manuscripts. Some of them he is supposed to have received from a congregation of Augustinians who had settled in an abbey near Oxford years before. Upon his death in September, 1632, he bequeathed 236 of them to Sir Kenelm Digby, who had studied under him at Oxford from 1618 to 1620, and whom he regarded as the infant prodigy of his era. Digby was then in the midst of a romantic career in which he later figured prominently, first on one side and then on the other of the religious conflicts which led up to Cromwell's accession to power. Already he had traveled and become widely known abroad; he had been knighted by James I and, with the King's approval, had achieved success as a privateer, after which he had been made a naval commissioner. The collection apparently was not of great interest to him, for in that same year he gave it to the Bodleian Library, which had been founded at Oxford in 1602. There, as the Digby Collection, the manuscripts took the name of the donor instead of the collector, and remained in inconspicuous seclusion for two hundred years.

Next comes the French Revolution, when Gervais Delarue, a French historian and authority on Norman and Anglo-Norman literature, took refuge in England. Before he returned to France in 1798 he examined a great number of original documents—among them, a dilapidated parchment on which had been transcribed a copy of the Chanson de Roland. In 1834, one year before he died, he published three volumes of essays on Norman and Anglo-Norman bards, jongleurs, and trouvères, in one of which he copied some portions of that transcript. Little attention was paid to it until Francisque Xavier Michel, an antiquarian whom the French government had sent to England in 1833 to pursue his studies, published the complete text in 1837.

The manuscript became known as the Oxford Manuscript (Digby 23), and during the next hundred years a great number of books and articles were written about it, chiefly by French, German, and Italian commentators. The consensus is that it was written by an Anglo-French scribe, between 1140 and 1170, in the French dialect spoken in England after the Norman Conquest. No other copy of it, or of the original Chanson, except the recensions referred to above, has been found. As Prof. Luquiens remarked in his Introduction to the *Three Lays of Marie de France*, "not much but Latin was considered worthy of parchment" in those days. Also it seems to be the generally accepted belief that the so-called Baligant episode, a sort of sequel to the Roland Song which takes up most of the last third of the Oxford Manuscript, was not a part of the original Chanson but an interpolation written by a different author. Essentially it is a song of Charlemagne, containing wholly apocryphal descriptions of his battle with and defeat of the Emir of Babylonia after the death of Roland and his comrades. It is markedly inferior in style and is tiresomely drawn out. Interwoven as it is in the Oxford Manuscript, it is repetitious and interrupts the coherence and dramatic development of the whole.

Some of the commentators, conscious of what they conceived to be defects and gaps in the Oxford Manuscript, undertook to reconstruct the lost original of the Chanson from some of the recensions. Their suggested emendations were examined by Prof. Luquiens in a scholarly and convincing article, "The Reconstruction of the Original *Chanson de Roland*." * He concluded by recommending adherence to the Oxford Manuscript because of its perfection of "unity, coherence and emphasis" and "its artistry of balance" despite an occasional and readily explainable defect.

In form the Chanson was written in "laisses" (stanzas) ranging from five to thirty-four ten-syllable lines. The lines are not rhymed, but the last words of all the lines of a laisse are assonant. In French, assonances wherein the last accented vowel of one word is similar in sound to that of another although the consonants and number of syllables may be different (e.g. *ombre, hommes, contes, respondet, Saragossa*) are so common

* *Transactions,* Connecticut Academy of Arts and Sciences, Vol. 15 (1909), pp. 111-136.

and so readily available that their use permits a freedom of expression approximating that of English blank verse.

The form of versification of the Oxford Manuscript, however, combined with the archaic and difficult dialect in which it was written, has made translation into English poetry very difficult. In part, as George Saintsbury * has put it, that is because "the obstacles to assonance in English, and its probable disagreeables, are many and various."

Later in the twelfth century the chanson writers began to use dodecasyllabic lines in rhymed couplets. Translations in that form, however, whether in hexameter or pentameter, have not proved satisfactory. In reading them they become singsong and tedious. Again to quote Saintsbury, "rhyme in any form alters and in the case of the longer laisses has a terrible tendency, both in French and English to 'overdraw the account.' "

Prose translations, while they can follow the French text with close verbal accuracy, cannot reproduce any of the music of the Chanson. They do not sing. They fail to "recapture the first fine careless rapture" of the French trouvères.

Perhaps the reason why the Song of Roland is so little read nowadays is that the difficulties of translation have been such that there has not hitherto been any English version which adequately conveys the beauty, coherence, and dramatic power of the French.

* Note on Technique, accompanying Scott Moncrieff's translation.

In the New York Public Library are catalogued eight English translations, two in prose and six in verse. Of these, only the two in prose and one in verse are now in print and obtainable from the publishers.

The translations in prose tell the story well enough, but the poetry is not there. Furthermore they suffer from inclusion of the tiresome Baligant episode. Doubtless they are of value to the student; but there is in them no joy of reading.

The one available verse translation * is said to have been "done into English in the original measure," and is in ten-syllable assonant lines. Scott Moncrieff, the translator, describes it as "an attempt to reproduce line for line, and, so far as is possible, word for word, the Old French which lay dormant for centuries in the Bodleian Library at Oxford." Saintsbury's accompanying Note on Technique begins by expressing his early impression that "a satisfactory modernization or translation of 'the Chanson de Roland' was so difficult as to be nearly impossible and that such an enterprise in English was the darkest tower of all." His conclusion is that Scott Moncrieff has "managed the stumbling blocks . . . with a most creditable amount of skill and courage and with a very considerable success" but "has not wholly converted me." Nevertheless he commends the translation because it seems to him to be, "not merely

* *Song of Roland*, done into English in the original measure by Charles Scott Moncrieff, with an Introduction by G. K. Chesterton and a Note on Technique by George Saintsbury (London, Chapman & Hall, 1919—New York, Dutton, 1920).

in detail but in general effect, the most faithful version I have ever seen" of the great Song of Roland. As such it would seem to be of a considerable academic value.

From the viewpoint of the general reader, however, the reiteration in each laisse of a number (in some cases over thirty-two) of attempted English assonances, many of which are of the kind that Saintsbury calls "probable disagreeables," does not make for attractiveness. A more important defect is that the translator's effort to make each line end in an assonance frequently compels an unharmonious choice and arrangement of English words. Too often overstress on the letter crushes out some of the spirit. And here too the interpolation of the irrelevant Baligant episode, which adds some 1,600 lines to the 2,400 in the original Chanson, unduly lengthens the whole and is detrimental to its readability.

An excellent translation made by Leonard Bacon, a well known poet in his own right, was published by the Yale University Press in 1914 in a limited edition of which only a few hundred copies were distributed. It is not marred by overstringent literalism; but Bacon hampered himself somewhat by using rhymed couplets and also made what seems to me to be the mistake of including the Baligant interpolation. However that may be, it has been out of print for many years. The same is true of the other four earlier, and for various reasons inferior, translations into English verse.

Clearly, if this grand old French song is to come into its own among English-speaking peoples, it needs a new translation: one which will adequately show forth the essential poetic and dramatic spirit of the original.

To make such a translation Prof. Luquiens was exceptionally qualified by nature and training. Before writing "The Reconstruction of the Original *Chanson de Roland*" and his *Three Lays of Marie de France*, he had published in *An Introduction to Old French Phonology and Morphology*, a scholarly study of the changes which had taken place from the seventh century through the twelfth in the spelling and vowel and consonant sounds of French words and in the regular and irregular verb forms. In an appendix he showed, by phonetic symbols, how the quaint words in the first nine lines of the Oxford Manuscript of the Chanson de Roland would be pronounced in modern French.

Later he became interested in the science of versification, made investigations into the rhythm of Spanish and Italian verse and conducted experiments in verse reading with native experts. Probably that training, combined with his native poetic instinct, made him realize that the eloquence of the French Chanson could best be reproduced in unrhymed iambic pentameter. Doubtless, too, he had learned in his college classrooms that no line-by-line and word-for-word dictionary translation could turn an ode of Horace into an English poem. His thorough knowledge of the Old French in which the Chanson was written and of the spirit of the era during which it was being developed enabled him, with entire fidelity to the essential meaning of the original, to make such minor departures from the strict letter as would make it possible to transmute the music of this grand old Chanson into fluent English poetry.

And so, goddess-given by the muses of epic poetry and history, we have this new translation; one which, I trust, will at last make the Song of Roland as widely read and known as it deserves to be.

June, 1952   NATHAN A. SMYTH

prologue

    Charles the great King, lord of the land of France,
Has fought beyond the hills for seven years,
And led his conquering host to the land's end.
There is but one of all the towns of Spain
Unshattered—grim Saragossa, mountain-girt,
Held by Marsila, King of Spain, of those
Who love not God and serve false gods of stone
Brought from the shores of Araby.—Hapless King!
Your hour is come, for all your gods of stone!

the council of marsila

In Saragossa, under the green boughs
Of olive trees, the Paynim King in fear
Crouched on a splendid terrace of blue stone,
Around him all his court. And thus he cried:
"Woe unto us! Woe to the land of Spain!
Charles the great King from his dear France has come
To bring us fire and sword. I have no host
To match with his; against his fearful men
No men of mine can stand. Now counsel me,
And save me from dishonor and from death."

Blanchandrin, oldest knight of all the court,
And bravest, ever first to serve his King,
Uprose, and spake: "Be not dismayed, my lord.
Convey to Charles, the arrogant, the fierce,
A covenant of service and of love.
Send to him bears, and lions, and hunting-dogs,
And seven hundred camels, and beside
A thousand moulted hawks. Silver and gold
Spare not. Send him enough to cart away
In fifty wains; and with it may he glut
His hirelings. Long enough has he made war
In this our land. Let him return to Aix,
And you shall follow him at Michaelmas,
With purpose to receive the Christian faith,
And swear yourself his liegeman. If he ask

For hostages, O King, our dearest sons
Shall go, mine own among them, though they die.
For it is better they should lose their lives
Than we the land of Spain. We must not sink
To mean estate, and everlasting shame."

And then he said: "By this my good right hand,
By this my long white beard, the accursèd Franks
Will turn them quickly to their land of France.
And when they sit in their own homes, when Charles
Has thanked his Christian God in his own church,
At Michaelmas will he convoke his court. And then
The appointed day shall come, and the night come—
While we come not. So shall his heart be hardened,
And our dear sons shall die. And yet, O King,
Is it not better they should lose their lives,
Than we bright Spain the beautiful, and sink
To low estate and shameful servitude?"
And all the Paynims answered: "This is truth!"

And so the council ended. But the King
Called to him Clarin of the eastern march,
Priam, and Garlan of the long black beard,
And others of their kind, cunning as they,
Among them grey Blanchandrin, ten in all,
The ten most wicked of his wicked host,
And said to them: "Find out this Frankish King
Who sits before the walls of Cordova,
Take you the green-leaved olive in your hands,

Token of peace. And if, when you return,
Your several wisdoms have achieved our end,
The guerdon shall be silver and red gold,
And lands and fiefs as many as you will."
And all the Paynims answered: "It is well."

The council ended. But the Paynim King
Spake to his men: "Find out this haughty Charles
With olive branches, tokens of good will.
On suppliant knee entreat him, in the name
Of his own God, to end this cruel war.
And ere this present moon is dim, shall I
Come to his court, with all my chiefest lords,
From his own hand receive the Christian faith,
And offer him our fealty and love.
Our hostages await his word." He spake.
Blanchandrin answered: "We shall bargain well."

And so the Paynim called for ten white mules,
Whiter than milk, the gift of a rich king,
With silver saddles and with reins of gold.
The chosen Paynims mounted them, and rode
With branches of the olive in their hands,
And came to Charles. Though King of France, and strong,
His strength will not avail against their guile.

the embassy

Charles the great King was that day light of heart,
For Cordova had fallen. He had broke
With catapults her towers and strong walls,
And given rich booty to his men, their fill
Of gold and silver and dear accoutrement;
And not a Paynim lived to tell the tale,
For those who were not dead had been baptized.
The King had sought the shade of a deep wood,
And with him Roland sat, and Oliver, friend
Of Roland, plighted friend for life or death,
And many others of the Franks of France,
On Persian carpets lying. Some of them
Were playing draughts to while the hours away,
And others chess, while games of fence engaged
The younger men and nimbler. In the shade
Of a tall tree, beside an eglantine,
Uprose a throne of purest gold, and there
The great King sat who held sweet France in sway.
White was his beard and all snow-white his hair,
In face and form the noblest of them all.
If any man would find the King, there needs
No guide. The messengers dismount, and kneel
Before his throne, and greet him with soft words.

And first Blanchandrin rose, and said to Charles:
"King of the Franks, be yours the grace of God;
That God whom all should serve. Marsila sends

His greetings to you, and he bids you know
That he has put away his gods of stone.
And of his chattels will he give good measure:
Lions and bears, and hunting-dogs in leash,
And camels, and swift hawks, silver enough
And gold to burden half a hundred wains—
Enough to pay your men for the hard years
In Spain. All-powerful King, you are too long
In our fair country. Turn again to France,
And we shall be your servants." Thus he spake,
And the great King gave thanks to God in heaven
Then bowed his head in silence, answering not.

　　Long time he sat in silence, letting not
His words outrun his judgment. But at last
Lifted his head, and then his glance was keen
And fearful. "Ay, your promises are fair.
But ever has your master been my foe,
And for these honeyed words of yours, what pledge
Have I?" And grey Blanchandrin answered, saying:
"A score of hostages, mine own dear son
Among them, yours for life or hideous death,
And even nobler sureties, an you will.
And when, at home once more, you celebrate
The feast of your Saint Michael, him who saves
From peril of the sea, my King himself
Will follow you to Aix, and be baptized,
In your own fonts receive the Christian faith."
And Charles made answer: "So shall he be saved!"

ROLAND AND GANELON

The eventide was fair, and the sun sank
In glorious brightness. And the mules were stabled,
And stretched a tent beneath the trees, where slept
The Saracens till day dawned bright again.
And with the sun awoke the King, and first
Heard mass and matins; then beneath a pine
Summoned his wisest knights to counsel him.

Under a pine tree, where his golden throne
Was placed, he called his bravest knights together.
And first the Archbishop Turpin came, and then
Gerin and Gerier, Tybalt—he of Rheims—
And many more as brave and wise as they;
And likewise Roland came, and at his side
His comrade Oliver. Ay, and with the rest
Ganelon came, the traitor. So began
The fateful council, fraught with woe for France.

And the King spake, and said: "Fair sirs, to us
The Paynim sends his messengers, with store
Of precious gifts, lions and shaggy bears,
Camels and falcons, mules weighed down with gold
Of Araby—more than we may take away
In fifty of our wains. But he demands
We turn again to our own land, and he
Will follow us straightway, and there subscribe

In all things to our law and glorious faith,
Turn Christian, be my liegeman—ay, and yet
I fathom not his real intent." He spake,
And the Franks cried: "It is a trap—take heed!"

The King had spoken, but in sudden wrath
Sprang Roland from his place, and cried aloud:
"In evil hour, O Charles, do you confide
In Marsila. Seven years have you made war
In Paynim Spain—while I have won for you
Many a strong-walled town—and seven years
Has Marsila played the traitor. Once before
Came heralds like to these, with olive boughs,
Who snared you then as these would snare you now:
For then, as mayhap now, your Franks were moved
To give you foolish counsel, for they said
'Send Basil, and send Basan, to the King.'—
He hanged them on the barren, wind-swept hills
Of Saragossa. Nay, this war must end
As it began, O King, with fire and sword.
On, then, to Saragossa—sit you down
Before her obdurate walls for aye, if need.
Avenge the blood of them the traitor slew!"

And the great King was silent, answering him
Nor good nor ill, and fingered his white beard.
The Franks were silent all, till Ganelon strode
Before the throne, and raised his voice, and said:
"Woe unto you, O Charles, if you believe

A fool—or me or any other man—
To your own harm. When now the Paynim King
Makes known that he will join his hands, and swear
To be your liegeman, hold all Spain in fief,
And follow evermore our Christian faith,
Who counsels you that we should say him nay
Cares little how we die! It is not right
That counsel born of arrogance should thrive.
Turn we from fools, and hold with prudent men!"

Then aged Naimon, wisest of the Franks,
Uprose and spake: "O Charles, with words of gold
Has Ganelon spoken, for the Paynim King
At last is vanquished utterly. You have wrung
His castles from him, and your catapults
Have broke his strongest walls. His towns are burned.
His men are dead. If now he asks for peace,
You should not heap upon him heavier woes.
When now he grudges not his hostages,
It is not right to urge this cruel war."
And the Franks answered: "This is truth, O King."

And the King said: "Whom shall we send, fair sirs,
To Saragossa?" And Naimon spake again:
"Send me to Marsila. Give to me your glove
And herald's wand." But Charles made answer: "Nay,
You are my wisest counsellor; you I need
At my right hand. The task is not for you."

And the King spake: "Whom shall we send, my lords,
To Saragossa?" And Roland quickly leapt
Before the throne. But Oliver laughed, and said:
"Your temper is too fierce; it would, methinks,
Embroil you in some mischief. An it please
The King, mine be the task instead." But Charles
Made answer: "Neither of you shall do this thing:
Nor you, nor other of the twelve great peers—
By this white beard I swear it." And the Franks
Were silent all, nor dared gainsay their King.

But then the Archbishop rose, Turpin of Rheims,
"Let be your peers, for they have toiled enough
In this accursed land. Give me your staff
And glove, and I shall seek the Paynim King,
Shall cunningly discern, mayhap, his heart
And real intent." But then again did Charles
Make answer, angrily: "Nay, you shall not go."

"My lords," so spake the King, "choose me a man
Fearless enough, and true." And Roland cried:
"Let it be Ganelon. He is valiant—ay,
And true." And straightway all the Franks approved
With a great shout. But Ganelon, leaping up
In sudden anger, throwing aside his cloak,
And standing forth in silken tunic, with hate
In his grey eyes, and yet so passing fair
That all wondered, cried unto Roland: "Fool!
Think not to hide your purpose! All men know

I am your stepsire, and for that alone
You hate me, and would send me into Spain.
If God permit that I return, I swear
To bring upon you great unhappiness,
Which shall endure through all your wretched life."
Then Roland: "You are mad! What all men know
Is this—that I care not for threats! But hold!
The King should send a prudent man. Stand back!
And let him give his glove and staff to me."

And Ganelon answered: "These are empty words,
For you are not my liegeman—nay, nor I
Your lawful lord, to bid you do my hest.
You may not go for me to the dread court
Of Marsila. Charles has spoken. I must go
To Saragossa.—Yea, but there shall I
Liefer some madness do, than not assuage
Mine anger." But Roland, hearing, laughed aloud.

And as he laughed, the heart in Ganelon's breast
Flamed with a sudden rage. He scarce could stand,
So swirled all sense within him. Then he cried:
"I hate you, Roland, hate you. You have brought
This cruel choice upon me, you alone.—
King of the Franks, I stand at your behest.

"I go to Saragossa.—They who make
That journey come not back to France. And so

Do you, O cruel King, lightly unmate
Your sister, whom you gave to me for wife,
So you make fatherless my son. To him
I leave my goods and fiefs. These mortal eyes
Shall never see him more." But Charles replied:
"Ganelon, tender of heart, it is for me
To bid you come or go, to obey is yours."

And the King said to Ganelon: "Stand you forth;
Be yours the staff and glove. Have you not heard?
The Franks entrust this embassy to you."
"Sire," cried the Count, "this thing has Roland done,
And for it shall I hate him alway, ay,
And Oliver, his friend, because he is
His friend; and the Twelve Peers, because they love him.
Here in your royal presence, Charles, I them
Defy! So let them look to their dear lives!"
But Charles replied: "Your rancor is too deep.
Yet must you go. It is your King's command."
"Yea, Sire, I go, but I shall not return—
Nor Basan nor his comrade did return."

And Ganelon, when the King held forth his glove,
Loath to obey, still hesitating, faltered—
From the King's hand it fell to earth. And then
The Franks were sore dismayed, crying: "What woe
Does this portend?" And Ganelon spake, and said:
"What this portends, you all shall know too soon."

And to the King he said: "If I must go,
Give me your leave to go straightway." And Charles
Made answer, saying: "I speed you in the name
Of Christ and of your King." Then signed he him
With the true cross, and gave him staff and script.

Then straightway Ganelon turned him to his tent,
And made him ready for the irksome road
With dear accoutrements. He girt his sword,
Fastened upon his feet spurs of bright gold,
Mounted a steed of war. And then, my lords,
Might you have seen the weeping of strong warriors,
Who said to him: "Alas for you, O Count!
Long have you dwelt in the King's court, but none
Has ever done you insult till this day.
He who adjudged this embassy to you
Shall not be shielded even by Charles the King.
Better for Roland had he voided spite
On lesser men than you." And then they said:
"Sire, take us with you." But he answered them:
"Nay, God forfend. I shall not lead my friends
To death. Into sweet France shall you return,
To greet my wife for me, and Pinabel
My truest friend, and Baldwin my dear son,
Whom you shall ever hold for your liege lord."
And, saying thus, he fared upon his way.

Under an olive tree he overtook
The Saracens, and rode with them. But soon
He and Blanchandrin fell behind a space,
And spoke each to the other cunning words.
Blanchandrin first: "A wondrous man your Charles,
Whose conquering host has entered every land,
And sailed to Britain over the salt sea,
Therein to levy tribute for Saint Peter.
What does he want of us in this our Spain?"
The other answered, saying: "Such is Charles,
And none on earth may stand against his will."

Blanchandrin said: "The Franks are valiant men
And true; and yet, methinks, they do not love
Their own liege lord, when thus they counsel him.
To him and others shall they bring confusion."
And Ganelon answered: "Nay, there is but one
Shall be confounded—Roland. Yester morn
The King of France was sitting in the shade
Of leafy trees, and Roland came, steel-clad,
Fresh from the sack of Carcassonne, and held
In his right hand a scarlet apple. 'Lo,
Fair sir,' quoth he, 'I give you here the crowns
Of all the Kings of earth.' But his great pride
Shall yet destroy him, for he plays each day
With death. And when he dies, we shall have peace."

Blanchandrin said: "He is a fearful man,
This Roland, who would glut him with the cries
Of cringing kings through all the world. But stay—
What men will aid his madness?" And again
The other spake: "The Franks do love him so
That they will never fail him, for he pours
Silver and gold upon them, steeds of war,
And rich accoutrement. It is not strange
That Charles himself so loves a man who swears
To give him the great world from East to West."

So spake the twain together, cunningly,
Till each to other pledged his knightly word
To compass Roland's death. Then they rode on,
Whether by shady path or white highway,
To towered Saragossa, and drew rein
Under a green yew tree. There stood the throne,
Covered with Alexandrine silks, whereon
Sat Marsila, King of Spain, and all about
His Saracens were standing. Ay—but none
Did speak, or hardly breathe, so keenly strained
Was every ear to know the fateful tidings.
And lo—Blanchandrin came, and the strange Frank.

And straightway grey Blanchandrin took the hand
Of Ganelon, while the twain in sight of all
Stood forth. Then first the Paynim spake, and said:
"Greeting, O Marsila, in Mahomet's name,
And great Apollin's! We have done your hest.

To Charles we gave your messages of peace,
Who lifted up his hands and praised his God,
But answered us no other word. Here stands
His chosen herald, Ganelon, knight of France.
From him shall you receive, O King, or peace
Or war." And Marsila answered: "Let him speak."

And so the Frank, who had considered well
How he should do, began with dexterous words,
And said: "Greeting, O Marsila, King of Spain,
And God be with you alway, the true God
Whom all should serve. This is the word of Charles
Of France: 'If you turn Christian, half of Spain
Is yours in fief; if not, you shall be seized
And bound, whether you will or not, and brought
To Aix in France, there to be tried and judged,
There to be slain in shame and vile estate.' "
He spake, and the King flushed, and in his grasp
Trembled an arrow feathered with pure gold.
But, ere it flew, Blanchandrin stayed his hand.

The Paynim's face was flaming like a fire.
He shook the poisoned shaft. And so the Frank,
Drawing his sword the length of fingers twain
From out the sheath, spake to it lovingly:
"O shining blade and true, long worn and wielded
In presence of great kings, be it not said
My death was lonely—nay, the richest blood
Of heathen Spain shall this day ransom you."
But all the Paynims cried: "Let be this strife!"

The wisest Paynims pled, until the King
Sat him again upon his throne. And one
Said to him then: "O King, you bring great woe
Upon us, if you slay him. Nay, you must
In patience listen." And to him replied
The Frankish knight: "Good sir, I must endure
Your King's displeasure, yet not hold my peace
For all the wealth of Spain, for all the gold
That God has made. I must make known the word
Which Charles the Great, our glorious King of France,
Sends to his mortal foe, the King of Spain."
And then he cast aside his heavy cloak
Of marten, trimmed with Alexandrine silk,
Throwing it on the earth, and in his hand
Gripped by the golden hilt his sword. And so
The Paynims cried: "Here stands a valiant man!"

But Ganelon came where sat the King, and spake:
"Unjustly are you wroth with me, for I
Am but the unworthy messenger of him
Who governs France. To you he says, O King,
You must receive the Christian faith, and then
The half of Spain is yours; the other half
Shall be Count Roland's—" Here he laughed, and said:
"Forsooth, a gentle partner!" Then said further:
"If you refuse, your Saragossan walls
Shall not protect you. Nay, you shall be seized,
And bound, and brought to Aix. Nor will you ride

Or battle steed or ambling palfrey—nay,
A pack horse will you ride. And there in Aix
You shall be judged and hanged. And all these words
Are herein writ." He ended so, and laid
In Marsila's hand the script of Charles his King.

The Paynim's face with wrath burnt like a brand.
He broke the waxen seal, and looked upon
The written words within, and cried aloud:
"My lords, the Frankish Christian trusts me not
In my intent, bidding me not forget
Basan and Basil, heralds whom I slew
On the wild hills of Saragossa. Lo,
If I would save my kingdom, must I send
Mine uncle as a pledge, my chiefest lord,
Caliph of sea-girt Carthage!" But his words
Kindled the sudden anger of his son,
Who cried: "Enough of Basan and his friend!
Ay, true it is, we slew them, as again
We slay this Ganelon." And the Frankish knight,
Drawing his sword, brandishing it on high,
Set him against the trunk of a stout pine.

But Marsila turned him then to a deep grove
Of olive trees, and called his son and all
His wisest men to council. And first spake
Blanchandrin, saying: "Let the Frank be brought
Before you, King. He gave his knightly word

To help us somewhat." Marsila, quickly glad,
Gave his consent, and grey Blanchandrin took
The traitor by the fingers of his hand
And brought him so within the grove. And there
Was plotted the foul treason against France.

"Fair Ganelon," spake the Paynim King, "I did
You madness, when in anger uncontrolled
I would have slain you. Here I make amends
With these great furs of sable, worth their weight
In purest gold. Think you the gift too mean?"
And the Frank answered: "Nay, I take your gift,
And may almighty God repay it you."

And the King spake, and said: "O Frankish knight,
I have it in my heart to like you. Come,
Tell me of Charles the Great. I have heard say
That he is old, that he has worn his years,
Like a used garment, threadbare. He has seen
So many lands, so many blows has dealt,
Has brought to mean estate so many kings—
When will he tire of war?" The other then:
"Not yet! Whoever looks upon him, sees
The conqueror still. If I should him extol
Through all the day and night, till morrow's dawn,
I should not touch, methinks, the end of all
His worth, nor I nor any other man
More skilled in speech. God has illumined Charles
With name and fame not to be dimmed by time."

The Paynim answered: "Wonder fills my heart
For the great King, whose hair and beard are white
As driven snow, whose years are numberless.
But he has won so many lands, has turned
Upon his shield so many pointed spears,
So many kings has overthrown and slain—
When will he tire of war?" And the Frank said:
"It will not be, O King, while Roland lives.
From east to west there is no better knight
In the wide world, and Oliver his friend
Fights ever at his side, and the Twelve Peers,
And with them twenty thousand Franks, who make
Our vanguard alway. So the King is safe."

"Fair Ganelon, you have seen my gathered host—
Four hundred thousand men. Can they withstand
This Charles and his fierce Franks?" "Not they, O King,
For all their numbers. Nay. Let madness be,
And turn to wisdom. Send the King of France
Rich gifts to blind him, and to soothe him send
A score of pledges. Then shall he turn back
To his dear France, and in your realm of Spain
Shall stay his rear guard only. But, methinks,
The rear guard will not stay without Count Roland,
Nor he without his comrade Oliver—ay,
And they shall both be slain, or trust no more
In Ganelon. Charles at last shall see the end
Of his great pride. Then will he tire of war!"

"Soldier of France, how shall we be assured
Of Roland's death?" "Thus will it come to pass.
When Charles is far away, beyond the hills
Which sunder France and Spain, and shall have left
Roland behind him, and the peers of France,
With only twenty thousand men, then you
Shall fall upon them swiftly, with a host
Of countless thousands. Not one battle—sooth—
Shall vanquish Roland, nay, nor two, nor three,
While Franks and Paynims fall in fearful fight,
But in the end, however much he strive,
Death shall him seize, relentless, merciless death.
Then will you know the worth of steadfastness,
For then will Charles grow weary of this war.

"Were Roland dead through us, it were for Charles
As though a sword had severed his right hand.
It were the end of all his terrible host,
Which nevermore would be assembled—nay—
Your land would rest at last." And Marsila laughed,
And kissed the Frank, and bade a troop of slaves
Bring from his treasury bags of yellow gold.

And the King said: "Why waste the day in words?
Not countless words, but one true oath, may bind
Our purposes together. Will you swear
The death of Roland?" And the other cried,
"I swear," and swearing, kissed the hallowed hilt
Of his good sword, and turned him traitor so.

And Marsila bade his black-robed priests bring forth
A lettered book, wherein was writ the law
Of all his gods. He laid it on his throne,
And swore, kissing the dark, enciphered page,
The death of Roland: "Ay, if Roland stay
In our bright Spain, he dies." And Ganelon laughed,
As one who in some market bargains well.

And thereupon strode forth a Paynim knight,
Swart Valdabron, and laughed for joy, and said:
"Take you my trenchant sword, fair sir—and none
Was ever better; in the hilt doth gleam
The worth of many coins of purest gold.
I give it you against the glorious day
When you and I shall find the fearful Count
Among the rear guard." "You do not misplace
Your trust," the other answered, and the twain
Embraced each other, pledging so their faith.

Then Climborin, the Saragossan, came,
And laughed for joy, and said: "Warrior of France,
Take you my helmet—none in all the world
Is better—you shall help us rid the world
Of the mad Count." "Nor you unwisely place
Your trust," the other answered, and they kissed
Each the other on lips and bearded cheek.

Then came the Queen herself, fair Bramimonde,
And softly said: "Sir Knight, I love you well,

Seeing my sire and all his wisest men
Do love you. Lo, these bracelets of bright gold,
With amethyst and jacinth set, I send
To your dear wife. The twain may not be bought
With all Rome's wealth; their glittering stones
Will blind great Charles himself." And Ganelon took
The yellow rings, and thrust them in his boot.

And while they spake these friendly words, the King
Summoned his stewards, bidding them prepare
A princely gift for Charles. And they replied:
"Yea, seven hundred camels are prepared,
Laden with gold and silver, and a score
Of hostages, the noblest of the land."

And Marsila laid his hand upon the arm
Of the glad Frank, and said: "You are a man
Both brave and wise. I charge you by that God
Whom Christians worship, hold your faith with us;
Great store of treasure shall be yours, ten mules
Charged with Arabian gold, and every year
You shall receive a like reward. And lo,
Within your hand I lay the golden keys
Of Saragossa. Give them to great Charles,
Together with my gifts.—And then, good friend,
Then shall you bring to pass that Roland stay
To guard the rear; and when he is entrapped
In some deep gorge and dismal, he shall die."
And so the traitor, hiding not his joy,
Leapt on his horse, and turned him back to France.

The host of Charles the King was marching home,
And near the ruins of Valterne, whose walls
Roland aforetime shattered—with great blows
That felled them for an hundred years—they camped,
Waiting for Ganelon, whom the King had sent
To Spain. And in the crystal dawning, came
The traitor Count, and rode among the tents.

The King had waked betimes, and prayed to God,
And now was sitting where the springing grass
Was spread, a cloth of green, before his tent.
Roland was there, with Oliver his friend,
Naimon, and all the King's most trusted men
And tried. And there the traitor came, and spake
With cunning words: "God save you, gracious King!
Behold, I bring you here the golden keys
Of Saragossa, and great store of gifts,
And twenty hostages. True, I bring you not
The Caliph of great Carthage, of whom most
You were desirous. But the fault is not
Marsila's. Nay, these eyes did see the ships
Of the black Caliph sail away, with him
And all his men, their shining hauberks donned,
And helmets laced, and golden-hilted swords
Girt round them. So they fled the shores of Spain,
Filled with the fear of our baptismal fonts.

But ere they sailed four leagues, a tempest rose,
Which sank tneir ships, and drowned them in the waves
Of the blue sea; and that is why, O Charles,
I have not brought the Caliph. But I bring
The promise of King Marsila, who has sworn
That ere this present moon is dim, himself
Will come to you, from your own hand receive
The land of Spain in fief, and turn him Christian."
He spake, and Charles gave thanks to God in heaven,
And words of praise to Ganelon. And the horns
Of all the Frankish host rang out with loud
And joyous blare. The soldiers folded up
Their tents, and strapped on sumpters all their goods,
And gladly turned their faces to sweet France.

Charles the great King has wasted Spain, destroyed
Her castles, sacked her towns—and so he turns
In gladness homeward. Ay, on that same night
While the red sun was sinking, Roland climbed
A hill that looked on France, and planted there
The royal flag, pointing the next day's march
To all the impatient soldiers camped below.—
But, meanwhile, through the valleys all around
The Paynim hordes were swarming, armed for war,
Hauberk and helmet laced, and shield on shoulder,
And sword and spear in hand. And on that night
They hid them in the heart of a black wood,
Waiting the dawn, four hundred thousand strong,
Unseen, unheard—O God!—of all the Franks.

And while in utter stillness the night lay
Upon the hills, Charles dreamed he stood alone
In midst of fearful Pyrenean crags,
And Ganelon came, and from his trembling hand
Wrested his spear, and brandished it on high,
And lo! the ashen shaft shivered and sprang
To a thousand splinters—yet the King woke not.

So the night passed, and day dawned bright again;
And through the marshalled ranks of his great host
He rode, and cried: "Soldiers, against the sun
Rises the blessèd pass of Ronceval,
Winding across the hills to France. And whom
Shall we elect, my lords, to guard the rear?"
Then quickly Ganelon spake: "Let Roland stay
To guard the rear. For he over us all
Is brave." And suddenly flashed his fearful dream
Through the King's thought, and he cried out: "You **wretch!**
You devil more than man! what madness fills
Your heart? For none may lead in Roland's place
The vanguard, his of right." And Ganelon said:
"Let be, O King! What matters it who leads
Where lies dear France, and friends and hearth and home?"

But Roland, scarce the words were spoken, cried
With a glad heart: "Good stepsire, you I love
For giving me the rear guard. Charles the King
Will be content with me, for he will lose
Nor steed of war nor palfrey, nay, nor sumpter,

Which be not bought with Paynim blood." He spake,
And Ganelon curbed his spleen, and answered not.

And Roland said: "O King, give me the curving bow
Thou holdest—ay—and by that token give
The rear guard to me. None shall say—methinks—
I let it fall, as Ganelon let fall
Your glove." But the King wept, and sat a time
In troubled thought, and fingered his white beard.

Then stood forth Naimon, oldest of the Franks,
And wisest, saying: "You have heard, O King,
The angry words of Roland. There is none
May claim the rear guard now. Give him your bow,
And choose good men to aid him." And the King,
Shuddering, laid the bow in Roland's hand.

Then spake, saying: "Fair sir, fair nephew Roland,
The half of my great host shall stay with you.
In Ronceval." But Roland answered him:
"Nay, God destroy me if I now belie
My lineage. Twenty thousand men, mine own,
Shall stay with me. And you, O King, shall pass
Through the defiles in surety, fearing nought
While Roland stays behind in Spain, and lives."

So spake Count Roland, and upon his strong,
Swift courser sprang. But Oliver his friend
Came spurring to his side, and spurring came

Gerin and Gerier, Anselm called the Proud,
Berengier, and Girard of Roussillon,
Ivon and Ivor, Otto, and the Dukes
Of Gascony and Burgundy—the twelve
Great Peers of France. And then the good Archbishop,
Turpin of Rheims, held not his peace, but cried
That Roland needed—sooth—a man of God.
And so these stayed, with twenty thousand men.

The hills were high, and all the valleys filled
With fearful darkness. Through the grim defiles
The Franks crept slowly, with loud cries of toil.
But when at last they came where climbed the road
No longer, downward sloping to sweet France,
To the fair, flowered fields of Gascony,
Their hearts beat faster for the thought of home,
Of wife or sweetheart, and the eyes of all
Were dimmed with tears of gladness. The great King
Alone was sad, for Roland was afar,
In the defiles of Spain—and the King wept.

The twelve great Peers were far away in Spain,
With twenty thousand fearless men, and Charles
Was riding to sweet France. Over his face
He threw his cloak, and wept. Beside him rode
The aged Naimon, saying: "Why are you
Thus tearful, O my King?" And he replied:
"Alas, my sorrow is too great. I may
No longer hide it. France shall be destroyed

By Ganelon. Ay—for yesternight I dreamed
He plucked the ashen spear from mine own hand
And shattered it to splinters—and he it was
That gave the rear guard to Count Roland, whom
I leave behind in a strange land. O God!
If him I lose, whom have I in his stead?"

the paynim peers

And the King wept, and all his men were filled
With a great fear for Roland, lest his life
Be meanly sold for silver and for gold
By Ganelon, and garments of fair silk,
And horses, and strange beasts from overseas.—
And now the Paynim King, with hope renewed,
Had gathered fighting-men from every town
And furthest part of Spain, a fearful horde.
To Saragossa's highest battlement
They hoisted a stone god, and prayed. Then rode,
Each vying with the other, over hill
And through deep valleys, till they came at last
To Ronceval, and saw the banners flying
Of the twelve Peers of France. And then they knew
The hour of mortal combat was at hand.

Marsila's nephew, Adalroth, on mule
Ablaze with golden trappings, rode before
The Paynim King, and cried: "Fair uncle, Sire,
Long have I served you, suffering pain and toil,
Fighting for you on many fields, and now
I crave a boon—vouchsafe to me the blow
That kills Count Roland. Him shall I strike down
With this my spear, Mahomet aiding me,
And so set free the uttermost ends of Spain
From these high hills unto the western deep.

His King shall tire of war, and all the Franks
Shall yield them; you shall live in peace." He spake,
And Marsila gave to him his iron glove.

In his right hand he grasped and shook on high
The gauntlet, crying: "You could not bestow
A better gift. But there are twelve great Peers
Of France—twelve must there be of us." And first
The King's own brother, Falseron, came forth,
And said: "Fair nephew, I shall ride with you
This glorious day. And this day by our hands
The soldiers of great Charles shall be destroyed."

And then the fell Corsablis, wickeder
Than Marsila's wicked self, but brave—not he
Would flinch in fight for all the gold of God—
Came riding quickly, and beside him rode
His friend Malprimis, fleet of foot, who cried
Before the King: "On! On to Ronceval!
If Roland be in Ronceval, he dies!"

And then spake Clarin, ruler of the march
Of eastern Spain, a courteous man, and famed
For skillful fighting from the saddle—yea,
Were he a Christian, it were meet to praise
His knightlihood—who said: "In Ronceval
Shall I this day find Roland. He shall die,
And Oliver his friend shall die, and die
The twelve proud Peers, and all the accursèd Franks.

Charles the great King is old; he shall at last
Weary of war, and leave bright Spain in peace."
And his bold words brought joy to the King's heart.

And then stood forth the Prince of Morianne—
No crueller Paynim breathed in all of Spain—
And boasted he would lead to Ronceval
Full twenty thousand shields and spears, and when
He found Count Roland, death should find him too,
And Charles the King should never laugh again.

Then Turgis of Tortosa, gluttonous
For Christian blood, came running to the King,
Crying: "Be not dismayed. Mahomet helps
The faithful more than Roman Peter helps
These Christian dogs. In yonder Ronceval
This day shall I fight Roland, and from death
No saint shall save him. Mark you this my sword—
My long, keen sword! O, I shall measure it
With Durendal, and then shall all men know
Which of the twain is longer, keener—ay,
If these mad Franks be mad enough to stand
Against us, they shall die in utter shame,
And Charles shall nevermore wear golden crown."

Then strode the lord of far Valtierra forth
Before the King, and cried: "To Ronceval
I fare, and shall undo the arrogant pride
Of Roland. By this hand shall he be slain

In Ronceval, nor carry back to Charles
His madman's head, nor save his Franks from death
Sweet France shall be a wilderness, wherein
The voice of Charles shall cry for men in vain."

Then called the King to grim Estramaris
And grey Estorgant, standing side by side,
Companions old in villainy and crime:
"Stand forth, my lords, for you shall go with these
To Ronceval." And they replied: "Your words
Are good to hear, O King. We yearn to meet
This Oliver, this Roland, and the Peers.
Our blades are keen, and we shall crimson them
In good warm Frankish blood. The Franks shall die,
And Charles shall mourn, and we shall give to you
All France. If you will come to Ronceval,
Great Charles himself we twain shall give to you."

And running came fair Seville's noble prince,
Ruler of all the land that lay about
That city—ay, as far as the blue sea;
A handsome man, and one to win the hearts
Of all fair ladies. None could look upon
His winsome face, and straightway lighten not
With love—in very sooth, a knightly Paynim.
Into the throng about the King he came,
And cried in a loud voice: "Be not dismayed,
My lord, for I shall fare to Ronceval
And slay Count Roland, and Oliver his friend,
And the twelve Peers. O, how my fingers burn

About this golden hilt! This blade shall run
With crimson streams of blood from Frankish veins.
France shall be shamed, and old, white-bearded Charles
Shall never know another joyous day.
Ere one short year has passed, we shall have seized
All France, and we shall feast and make our beds
Under the roof of Charles' own church." He spake
And laughed, and gladness entered the King's heart.

And last came forth the ruler of that land
Men call the Hills of Darkness—a black gnome,
With raven hair that dragged behind him, gnarled
Like a dwarf oak, but strong enough to bear
A sumpter's burden. In that land—they say—
The sun shines not, nor rain nor gentle dew
Fall from the heavens, and not a grain of corn
May ripen; every stone is black, so black
That some men say the Devil put them there.
The hideous Paynim spake, and said: "O King,
My sword is girt. In yonder Ronceval
I pledge you I shall use it well. Let him
Of whom all speak, this valorous Roland, come
To stay the sport, and if this blade of mine
Break not his Durendal, trust me no more.
The Franks shall die, and France shall be forgot."
So spake he, and the chosen Peers of Spain
Stood forth, and called a hundred thousand men
To follow them. They rode to a black wood,
And there prepared them for the imminent strife.

the mаdness of Roland

The Paynims bound their coats of linkèd mail
About their shoulders, laced upon their heads
Their Saragossan helmets, girt their sides
With golden-hilted swords of shimmering steel
Forged in Vienna. Then they took their shields,
And slender lances of Valencian make,
Astream with pennons blue and white and red,
And all with a great shout leapt on their steeds
And rode in serried ranks, a fearful horde.
The day was clear, resplendent shone the sun,
Each several bit of armor flamed again.
And all the trumpets of the host rang loud;
The echoing rumor, borne on the west wind,
Found out the straight defile of Ronceval . . .
And then spake Oliver, saying: "Roland, friend,
We know that sound of old! The Saracens
Are near!" But Roland laughed, and answered him:
"God give your words be true! Then for our King
Here may we stand and fight as brave men should.
For his liege lord a knight ungrudgingly
Must bear distress and aching toil, nor shrink
From scorching sun or blast of winter wind,
Nor reck of life or limb. Soldiers of France,
Deal mighty blows, and so, when songs are sung,
This day's emprise shall not be held in scorn.

We fight for right, the Paynims fight for wrong!
And so, let come what may, we cannot yield!"

But Oliver climbed a lofty hill, and thence
Looked into Spain. Far, far away he saw
The host of Paynims riding. And he called
To Roland, saying: "Lo, from out of Spain
A fearful brightness comes—the blinding gleam
Of hauberks white and helmets all aflame
In the hot sun. Ay, Ganelon has betrayed
Us all, for he it was besought the King
To leave us here." But Roland answered him:
"Your words are madness, friend; it cannot be."

But Oliver climbed a high and jutting crag
Which looked toward Spain. There rode the Paynim host!
He saw the distant gleam of countless helms
Crusted with gold and set with priceless gems.
He saw the shining of bright shields, the hues
Of broidered coats of mail, and rows of spears
With pennons fluttering three-tongued from the tips.
Numberless was the host. He tried to count
The ranks, and could not. So, with hurrying steps
He turned him from the crag, and climbing down
Among the boulders, joined his friends again.

And then he cried: "From yonder pointed rock
I saw the Paynims riding. Never, I think,

Hath living man seen more of them. Alone
The vanguard rides a hundred thousand strong!
Shield upon shining shield they surge, as far
As eye can reach. Their helms and coats of mail
Are laced upon them. Heavenward point their spears,
The burnished tips bright-gleaming. Franks of France,
You shall have battle such as never was
Till now. Be strong in God! Nor yield of ground
The measure of this lance!" And all the Franks
Cried with one voice: "A curse on him who flees!
Not one of us will fail you in this hour!"

And Oliver cried to Roland: "The black host
Is numberless, and we, alas, are few.
Good comrade, wind your horn. The King will hear
The ringing blast, and turning back to Spain,
Will help us." Then did Roland answer him:
"Friend, I were mad to heed you. I should lose
The praise of men forever in sweet France.
Nay, I shall draw my sword, and steep the blade
In Paynim blood up to the hilt. Fore God!
The Paynims shall not thrive in Ronceval!
I pledge you, comrade, they shall die this day!"

"Roland, dear comrade, wind your ivory horn!
And Charles, though far away in France, shall hear,
With all his host shall come to succor us."
But Roland answered, saying: "God forbid
That I bring low my kindred, or become

-38-

The instrument of my dear land's dishonor.
Nay, rather shall I draw my sword, my tried
And trusted Durendal, and you shall see
Drenched in red blood the gleaming blade thereof.
The wretched Paynims here in Ronceval
Shall meet their doom—I pledge you, they shall die!"

"Roland, dear comrade, wind for us your horn!
The King will hear, and—this do I pledge you—
Will come to us." But Roland: "God forfend!
No living man shall say I winded horn
For Paynims! Such indignity shall not
Abase my kindred! When the fight is on,
Mine arm shall tire not. Nay, for you shall see
The steel of Durendal adrip with blood.
The Franks are soldiers good and true; their foes
Are doomed—yea, here in Ronceval they die!"

But Oliver said once more: "Let be, dear friend,
For I have seen the Paynims. Over hill
And wide-stretched plain they swarm. The stranger host
Is numberless, and we, all told, are few."
But Roland answered: "All the more I thirst
For battle, praying God that glorious France
Shall never lose through me her proud estate.
Ay, even death were sweeter than long life
Of utter shame, without the King's great love—
And he loves best a giver of stout blows."

Roland is brave. His friend is brave—and wise.
Both are good knights and true in word and deed.
Nor Oliver will yield him, though he die,
After the fight is on. And while they spake,
They heard the onrushing Paynims. Near at hand
Their battle cries rang loud. And Oliver said:
"Behold, proud Roland, where they ride. But Charles
Is far away. You would not wind your horn,
Hearkening not our prayers, and now we die
Unaided. Yonder, in the pass, our men
Prepare them for the strife, but sadly. None
Shall fight again." But Roland answered him:
"Enough! I know the heart within your breast
Is not turned craven. Stand we side by side,
And handle well our swords, let come what may."

And Roland, fearless as lion or leopard brought
To bay at last, called to the men of France
With words inspiriting. Then once more replied
To Oliver: "Friend, of this no more! for here
In Ronceval are twenty thousand Franks,
But not one coward. It is Frankish law
That every man must suffer for liege lord
Or good or ill, or fire or wintry blast,
Ay, truly, must not reck of life or limb.
Bestir you, comrade! Grasp your lance, and I
My Durendal, bestowed by the King's hand.
Whoever wears it after me shall say:
'This was the sword of one who fought till death.'"

Meanwhile Archbishop Turpin, he of Rheims,
Urging his steed with prick of spur, rode up
The mountain side a space, and from a rock,
As from a pulpit, called upon the Franks:
"Soldiers of France, when King Charles left us here,
He deemed us willing, in extremity,
To suffer death for his dear sake. Nay, more,
He deemed us soldiers of the Christian faith,
Willing to die for God. The hour of proof
Is come. The foes of Charles and God are here
Before you. Now confess your sins, and pray
God's bounteous mercy. Then shall I absolve you,
And if you die, the crown of martyrdom
Is yours, and yours great Paradise." He spake,
And so the Franks, dismounting, knelt them down,
And Turpin signed them with the cross of God,
And for a penance bade them deal stout blows.

The Franks arose with strengthened hearts, absolved
From sin, by Turpin signed with the true cross.
They leapt astride their chargers. Goodly knights
Were they, and armed as knights should be, and all
Athirst for battle. Then did Roland speak
To his dear friend: "O comrade, it is truth—
For gold and silver has my stepsire sold
The rear guard. Ay, the King of Spain hath made
A bargain for our blood. Come! Let us pay
The score with steel! Charles will avenge our deaths!"

And through the strait defile of Ronceval
He galloped, driving the spurs in his good steed.
His armor sat upon him pleasingly;
Within his iron grasp a splendid spear
Was brandished, pointing heavenward, and down
The shaft a pennon of pure white let fall
A fringe of gold across his hand. His face
Was laughing, as the face of one who goes
To dance, not die. And all the Franks acclaimed
Their leader. Roland, hearing, gave them thanks.
A gentle kindliness illumed the eyes
Which flashed a fearful wrath for Paynims. Then
He said: "Ride forward slowly, for the foe
Is coming fast enough to death. Shrink not
Before their spears, which soon shall be your own!"
And even as he spake, the rushing hosts
Were joining in the shock of mortal strife.

And Oliver said: "You winded not your horn,
And now we needs must fight our last good fight
Unaided. But the King is not at fault,
Nor they who, at his side, are going down
To France. Forward, my lords! Fight with the strength
Of desperate men, and stoutly give and take
The blows of battle, shouting the rally cry
Of the great King of France!" And so they cried
"Montjoy!" O, would you all had heard! for so
You never would forget what bravery
Is like! And then they charge—O God!

With what fierce pride! goading their horses' flanks
With frenzied spurs until they bleed again.
So rush to death. What else could brave knights do?
Nor do the Paynim hosts abate their speed.
Paynims and Franks—behold them joined in war.

And first rode forth from out the Paynim host
Marsila's nephew, Adalroth, with taunts
And threats. "O wretched men of France," he cried,
"This day you die, for he who should protect,
Has now betrayed you—ay—your King was mad
To leave you here in rock-bound Ronceval.
And now sweet France shall lose her fame, and Charles
His good right arm!" He spake, and Roland spurred
His eager, strong-limbed steed, and let him run—
O God, how fearful was his wrath!—and pierced
The Paynim's leathern shield and coat of mail
With his long spear. The pitiless point of steel
Entered his foe and passed through all his frame
Like flashing lightning, and his mortal soul
Fled shrieking through the wound. And Roland then
Hurled him from horse to earth, and brake his neck,
And cried: "You fool, Charles was not mad, I think,
To leave us here in Spain, nor played us false,
Nor glorious France shall lose her fame this day.
Comrades, lay on! for the first blow is ours!
We fight for right, these cowards fight for wrong!"

And then rode forth from out the Paynim host
Marsila's brother, Falseron—than he
No mortal man more ugly, with swart head

Of hideous breadth, his eyes a span apart.
But when he saw his nephew dead, his rage
Was fearful, and he rode without all curb
Against the Franks, shouting his battle cry
And threats of vengeance. Ay, but Oliver drave
Spur into steed, and charged with levelled lance,
And pierced the shield and hauberk of his foe,
So that the fringes of his gonfalon
Entered his frame, and from his horse he fell
Headlong to writhing death. And Oliver saw
The quivering corse lying, and said to it:
"Unglorious caitiff, little do I reck
Of all your threats. Lay on, soldiers of France!
This day we win or die!" And then he cried
"Montjoy!" the battle cry of Charles his King.

And then rode forth Corsablis, a fell king
From overseas, and shouted to his men:
"Surely this day is ours! The Franks are few,
And why fear we a few unfortunate Franks
Whom even Charles their King may not protect
From death?" He spake, and the Archbishop heard.
And hatred for the Paynim filled his heart,
And spurring with his golden spurs, he rushed
Upon him, brake his buckler, rent in twain
His useless hauberk, thrusting his heavy lance
Through flesh and bone and heart, and threw him down
Crashing headlong to death. And then he checked

The mad rush of his charger, turned about,
And, bending from the saddle, looked upon
The mangled corse, and cried: "What say you now?
Charles the great King is ever our defence.
It is not we who die like dogs this day,
But you and all your kind. Lay on, good Franks
Of France! Let none forget how men should fight!
For the first blow is ours by grace of God!"
And then he cried the rallying cry of Charles.

And Gerin smote Malprimis, whose thick shield
Availed him not a straw. The crystal boss
Flew to a thousand glittering bits, and so
The spear went crashing through, and through his coat
Of linkèd mail. The Paynim reeled, and fell
To death, and Satan seized his gibbering soul.

And Gerier galloped at his friend's right hand,
And slew Lord Clarin of the eastern march
Of Spain. Through shield and hauberk crashed unstayed
The cruel lance, and found the Paynim's heart,
And tore it from his breast. And Oliver cried
Across the field: "A merry fight is ours!"

Then Samson slew the Prince of Morianne,
Breaking his buckler bright with flowers of gold,
And driving half a spear shaft through his lungs
And wicked heart. And then across the field
The Archbishop cried: "A goodly thrust, my lad!"

Then Anselm gave the reins to his good steed,
And like a sudden hurtling thunderbolt
Fell upon Turgis of Tortosa, brake
His armor, pierced his frame, and cast him down
To death. And Roland cried, above the noise
Of the grim strife: "A goodly blow, fore God!"

And the bold Duke of Gascony drave spur
Into his horse, and gave him rein. He smote
The lord of far Valtierra, shattering shield
And futile hauberk with a blow that shook
The battlefield, and from the saddle fell
The dead man swirling, while the other cried:
"Caitiff, for you is no escape from hell!"

And Otto slew Estorgant with his lance
Of tempered steel. The Paynim's painted shield,
Half white, half red, availed him naught, nor yet
His broidered hauberk; nay, the iron spear
Rent both in twain, and from his plunging horse
The dead man toppled, while the other jeered:
"For you are gaping wide the doors of hell!"

But then Berengier smote Estramaris,
And slew him in the midst of the wild strife,
And so were left, of all the Paynim Peers,
Only that hideous gnome who ruled the land
Men called the Hills of Darkness, and the Prince
Of ancient Seville—these alone were left.

The Prince of ancient Seville, a brave knight,
Handsome and fleet of foot and strong, gave rein
To his good steed, and rushed on Oliver, brake
His jewelled shield under the boss of gold,
And would have pierced his hauberk, had not God
Turned the sharp lance aside. The straining shaft
Shattered to bits, and Oliver sat unshaken.
Then of a sudden surged the tide of war
Betwixt the twain, and swept them far apart.

The strife was fearful now, and in the thick
Fought Roland, sparing not his blows. At last
His lance brake short. He drew his trenchant sword,
His trusted Durendal, and spurred apace
On the swart gnome who ruled the Hills of Darkness.
Him did he smite, and the keen blade cut through
The Paynim's helmet, through his matted hair,
Down through his head and black, misshapen frame,
Rending his hauberk like a rag, and through
The golden saddle, slaying horse and man
With one great blow. The Paynim fell, and lay
Upon the thick, green grass, and Roland cried:
"Craven, by such as you this fight shall not
Be won. It was unwise for you to leave
Your sulphurous hills. Mahomet aid you now!"

And Roland rode where fiercest raged the fight,
Hewing the Paynims down with the bright blade

Of Durendal. O, would you all had seen
The good knight hurl them, each on other, dead.
The warm blood crimsoned both his arms, and bathed
The shoulders of his horse. And Oliver fought
As well as he, and the twelve Peers fought well,
And all the Frankish knights. And Turpin's voice
Rang clear and strong above the clash of arms,
Crying "Montjoy!" the battle cry of Charles.

Amid the weltering battle Oliver rode.
His lance was broken, yet with the blunt shaft
He fought unceasingly, and gave great blows
Heavy with death, until the shaft itself
Was splintered to his fist. But Roland cried:
"Let be, good friend. I like not quarterstaves
When iron and bright steel should swing and flash.
Where is your golden-hilted Halteclere?
Where hides your good, keen sword?" And Oliver laughed,
And said: "Good Roland, when may I find time
To draw it? nay—the fighting is too good!"

So spoke he, jesting. Then drew Halteclere,
And while his comrade looked flashed it on high,
And clove a wretched Paynim with one stroke
Asunder. And Roland laughed aloud, and said:
"Now do I you to brotherhood receive—
That is a blow the King would love!" And then
Through all the slaughterous field they cried "Montjoy!"

And so the battle raged, while Oliver smote,
And Roland rested not, but hewed great rings
Of crimson death about him. At their side
Fought the Archbishop, and the twelve great Peers,
And all their men laid on as brave men should,
Slaying the foes of God by hundreds—nay—
By tens of hundreds, till the frighted horde
Fled shrieking from the field, and so the Franks
Had respite. Ay—but what shall it avail?
Their hours are numbered now. They shall not see
Their kindred more, nor the great King, who waits
Across the mountains, waits and hopes in vain—
And meanwhile, far away in France, a storm
Of rushing wind and thunder swept the land,
And rain and hail were mingled, and the earth
Trembled, and over all was fearful darkness,
Save when the sky was split by thunderbolts.
From Xanten to Saint Michael of the Sea,
From east to west, there is no house in France
Unshaken, and men cry: "It is the end!
The end of all the world!" They do not know
The truth. Alas! It is the sorrowing
Of land and sea and sky for Roland's death!

the second battle

The Franks had held the field with heart and hand
Untiring. An hundred thousand foes had charged,
And scarce two thousand fled. And Roland spake,
Saying: "The men who fight this fight are good
And true. There is no king in the wide world
Has better men, and therefore is it writ
In Frankish story that our King is great."
But even while he spake, and while his Franks
Sought for their dead or dying through the field,
Weeping for friends or kindred, a new horde
Of Paynims came, led by the King himself.

Up through the valley came the embattled host
Of Marsila, King of Spain. Their helms of steel
Were tied with leathern latchets, on their arms
Their shields were fastened, and upon their frames
Lay hauberks broidered with bright golden threads.
And seven thousand horns winded the charge,
So that the noise thereof was heard afar.
And Roland spake to Oliver, saying: "Comrade,
It is the end. The traitor has made good
His promises of death. But the great King
Will take a mighty vengeance. Meanwhile, friend,
We shall have a battle; yea, and ruder far
Than we have ever seen. But I shall smite
With Durendal, and you with Halteclere.
In many countries have we wielded them,

And many battles won with them, and now
They must not give their names to shameful song!"

   The Paynim King had seen his people slain,
And, sounding horn and clarion, rode apace
To vengeance, leading a new host.—And first
Galloped a Paynim black as molten pitch;
No wickeder than he in all the swarm;
Spotted with many sins, believing not
In God, the Son of Mary; loving more
Treason and murder of his fellow men
Than good Galician gold; so fell that none
Had ever seen him laugh or play; but bold,
And so by Marsila loved, who this day laid
His flag, a painted dragon, in his hand.
And the Archbishop, seeing, loved him not
With Christian love, but yearned to smite him, thus
Communing with his heart: "The wretch, methinks,
Is far the worst of unbelievers—yea—
If now I slay him I shall do no wrong.
Whatever tide, a coward love I not."

   And so the Archbishop Turpin led the Franks
Against the Paynim host, riding the steed
Of a great king whom he aforetime slew
In Denmark—swifter than wind, with little feet
And slender legs, but strong, short thighs, wide croup,
And lofty back, with yellow mane and head,
Whereon two tiny ears sat saucily.

On him the good Archbishop rode to meet
The leader of the Paynims, on whose arm
Was fastened a round shield ablaze with gems
From overseas—a demon fashioned it
In some dark cavern, far from haunts of men.
But Turpin smote, and when his blow had split
The splendid buckler, it was little worth.
And the swart Paynim, riven clean in twain
By that one stroke, fell dead upon the field.
Then cried the Franks: "Here is true knightlihood!
In the Archbishop's hand the Cross is safe."

But when the Franks beheld the Paynim hordes
On every side, and hiding the green grass
Utterly, cried they out in sudden dread
To Roland, and to Oliver, and the Peers.
But Turpin bade them think no craven thought,
Nor yield an inch of the red field, lest men
Sing shameful songs thereof. "Much better die
In fight," he said. "And die we must. This day
Shall be our last in life. But of one thing
May I be surety—blessèd Paradise
Is opened wide for you, and with the Saints
Shall you be singing ere the sun hath set."
And when they heard, the Franks forgot straightway
The fear of imminent death, and cried "Montjoy!"

And then advanced a Saragossan Lord,
Ruler of half the city, Climborin;

Who never fled for any man—the same
Who swore a pact with Ganelon, and kissed
The traitor's lips, and gave him his own helm
With jewels all aflame. And now he cried
That he would bring dishonor to sweet France,
And snatch the golden crown from Charles' own head.
Astride his battle steed called Barbamoor,
Swifter than swallow or grey hawk, against
The noble Duke of Gascony he rode,
And threw him down, and shouted to his men:
"It is not hard to slay these Christians—smite!
And break the press in twain." And the Franks cried:
"Woe unto us! there fell a valiant man!"

And Roland called to Oliver: "Look, dear friend,
The Duke of Gascony is dead." And he,
Crying, "God give me vengeance," turned upon
The boasting Paynim. Down crashed Halteclere,
And devils carried thence the shrieking soul
Of Climborin. But Oliver checked not
The rush of his wild steed. With impetuous rage
He slew yet others—ay, smote and unhorsed
Full seven more who never afterward
Did battle. And Roland laughed. "In very sooth," quoth he,
"My comrade is enangered! Better blows
Have I not dealt. For such good thwacking blows
The great King loves us dearly." Then he cried
In a loud voice: "Lay on, soldiers of France."

And then came forth swart Valdabron, the lord
Of many ships and strong, and feared by all
Who sailed the sea, whose godchild was the King.
He erstwhile took Jerusalem by craft,
And in the Temple slew the Patriarch
Beside the holy fonts. And he had sworn
Friendship with Ganelon, giving his good sword
And many golden coins. And now he sat
His dappled war horse Grammimond, and rode
Swifter than falcon flies, defying forth
Samson the Duke. Him smote he with his lance
And hurled him from the saddle, shouting loud:
"Strike! for the day is ours!" And the Franks cried:
"Woe, woe to us! there fell a valiant man!"

But Roland, when he saw the warrior fall,
Was filled with fearful rage. He spurred where rode
The Paynim, shattered his bright helm, and split
The man asunder, for through helm and hauberk
Clove the sharp steel, and through the saddlebows
Deep in the war steed's back. So horse and man
Were slain at once, for naught could stay the hand
Of Roland. And the Saracens cried in turn:
"Woe, woe to us!" And Roland answered them:
"Yea, hated race, for yours is all the wrong!"

And one there was among the Paynim host
Whose armor, all of gold, outgleamed by far

The trappings of his mates; who came
From distant Afric shores where all the land
Obeyed his father. And he sat a steed
Called by a name which means "swift as the wind."
He rode and smote Count Anselm on his shield,
And cracked the red and blue, and rent in twain
His hauberk, thrusting so into his frame
The iron point, and then the wooden shaft.
And so the Count fell headlong, and was dead.
And the Franks cried: "Fate is unkind to us!"

But through the field Archbishop Turpin fared—
Never did priest sing mass, who with his hands
Did greater deeds in battle. And he cried
To the proud Paynim: "God shall give you death!
For you have slain my friend, and so my heart
Is broken." Wrathfully he rode, with lance
Levelled, and struck him down on the green grass.

Hard by another Paynim charged, the son
Of Cappadocia's King, upon a steed
High Marmorin, swifter than flying bird of prey,
Who rode on Gerin, and with well aimed spear
Shattered his crimson shield, and threw him dead
On a great rock. Then slew his comrade Gerier;
Berengier too; and many knights beside;
While all the Paynims shouted joyfully,
And the Franks cried: "Our bravest men are dead."

But Roland, when he heard the Franks make dole,
Thought that his heart would break for grief. He gripped
His bloody sword, and to the Paynim shouted:
"God give you death! for you have killed my friends.
And you shall pay in full for their dear lives."
He spurred his horse, eager no less than he,
And so the twain encountered face to face.

The Paynim was a valiant man and strong,
But when he came on Roland in his path,
And knew—although he looked upon him now
For the first time—that it could be no other,
He yielded him to fear, and turned in flight.
Which naught availed him, for Count Roland smote
So rudely that he split his helm, and clove
His nose and mouth and teeth, nor did the coat
Of shining mail stop the bright blade—it shore
The Paynim's frame asunder, and sank down
Into his steed, cutting the silver girths
Which held the golden saddle. Man and horse
He slew beyond all help. And so the host
Of Spanish Paynims wept aloud for grief;
And the Franks cried: "That was a goodly blow!"

And so the battle raged full wondrously,
While all the Franks with swords of gleaming steel
Laid on. Had you been there, you would have seen
A fearful sight, the dead and wounded thrown
One on the other, some with faces down,

And some with dying eyes turned heavenward.
No longer could the Saracens endure;
Whether they would or no, they fled the field,
And them the Franks pursued with might and main.

The battle raged full wild and wondrously.
In wrath the Franks fought on. They thrust and hewed,
And found, beneath the glittering coats of mail,
The flesh and bone. And the red blood ran down
On the green grass, and all the Paynims cried:
"We can no more endure. Great land of France,
Mahomet curse thee! Over other men
Thy men are brave!" So they made moan, and then
Cried with one voice to Marsila: "Come, O come!
And quickly, King, we need you lest we die!"

And Roland called to Oliver, saying: "Look,
The Archbishop handles lance and sword as well
As hallowed crosier." And his friend replied:
"In very sooth, the man of God shall teach
The men of battle." So the Franks fought on,
Though sore beset. Would you had seen the fight!
Would you had seen Count Roland and his friend
Smite with their swords! and with his pointed spear
The good Archbishop! Thousands did they slay—
So it is written in the Book of France—
Four battles did they fight, and win—the fifth
Went not so well. Alas, of all the Franks
Sixty alone are left, whom God has spared
Till now—and dearly will they sell their lives.

the horn

When Roland saw the men of France, or dead
Or dying, strewn on every hand, he spake
To Oliver his friend: "God save you, sir,
See you our comrades lying cold in death?
What woe is here for France the beautiful,
Of such men left forlorn! O Charles, great King
And friend, why are you not in Ronceval?
Oliver, comrade, how may we bring word
To Charles the King?" But Oliver spake, and said:
"Let be, good friend, I know not. Only this
I know—to yield us would be worse than death."

But Roland answered: "I shall wind my horn,
The King will hear it where he marches down
The strait defiles, and so—I pledge you, friend—
The Franks will turn them back." And Oliver said:
"Shame would it be for you, and lifelong shame
For all your lineage. When I pled with you
To call the King, you would not. Now, alas,
It is too late. The fight is on. If now
You wind your horn, it is not hardihood.
Too late! for both your arms are bathed in blood."
And he replied: "They have dealt winsome blows."

And Roland said: "The day is lost, but I
Shall wind my horn, and the great King will hear."

The other then: "It were not knightlihood.
I pled with you, and you, disdainful, spurned
My counsel. Now, with sword in hand, I call
Nor Charles, nor other men. Not his the blame,
Nor theirs who with him ride." And then he said:
"If God should give that ever I again
See my fair sister, Alda, this I swear—
Never shall you be held in her dear arms!"

And Roland cried: "Why are you wroth with me?"
The other answered: "Comrade, all the fault
Is yours. To temper knightlihood with sense
Is not unknightly; valor must be joined
With measure. Through your foolish arrogance
The Franks are dead, and nevermore will fight
For Charles. If you had given heed, the King
Would now be here. We should have fought and won.
Marsila, long ere this, were put to flight
Or slain. Roland, your reckless hardihood
Was fraught with woe for us. And now the King
Shall lose you, and your like shall never be
Unto the end of all things. You shall die,
And France shall be forlorn. This fearful day
Shall our dear friendship end, and the black night
Shall come upon us parted—and for aye."

But now the good Archbishop, hearing, drave
His spurs of purest gold into his steed,
And came where they contended, and spake thus,
Reproving them: "Sir Roland, ay, and you,

Comrade of Roland, in the name of God
Dispute not thus together. True, the horn
Will save us not. It is too late. And yet
It is the better way. Let the King come;
He will avenge us, and the Paynim hordes
Shall not turn joyous back to Spain. Our Franks,
Dismounting even here, will find us dead
And hewn asunder, but with gentle hands
Us will they lift on sumpters, while they weep
And call us by our names, and take us home
And bury us in some far church of France,
And we shall not be food for wolves or dogs."

He spake; and Roland winded loud and long
His ivory horn. Amid the towering hills
Echoed the flying sound. And Charles the King,
Full thirty leagues away, hearkened, and all
Who rode beside him hearkened, and he cried:
"Our men are fighting in far Spain!" and then
Spake Ganelon: "Nay, if other man than you
Should say it, we should laugh, and call him fool."

And Roland, with a wild and fearful blast
Winded his horn, so that his temples brake
And from his mouth leapt the bright blood. And Charles
Heard it, and all his soldiers, as they rode
Down to sweet France through valleys far away.
And the King cried: "It is the horn of Roland!
The Franks are fighting." And the traitor said:
"O King, your beard is white as snow, and yet

You prate like a foolish child. Do you not know
The arrogance of Roland? It is strange
That God hath suffered him so long. And once
He stormed a Spanish city in despite
Even of your command, and cruelly slew
The Saracens who sallied forth; then turned
The waters of the river from their bed
To wash the blood away, lest the fields prove
His disobedience. Why are you afraid?
Good God! for a rabbit would he wind his horn
The livelong day! And now he doubtless brays
For utter joy. What else? No mortal men
Would dare give battle to great Roland! Nay,
Ride on, O king, ride on! Why tarry here?
Ahead, and far away, lies the sweet land of France."

From Roland's lips flowed blood; his temples brake
With the wild blast and fearful. But the King
And all his soldiers heard it from afar.
And the King cried: "The blast is long and strong!"
And Naimon answered: "Ay, for a brave man
Is in distress, is fighting his last fight.
And he, O King, who bids you give no heed
Is he who has betrayed him. Arm yourself!
And cry your battle cry! And ride to help
Your kinsman Roland, for he needs you now."

And so the King drew rein, and loud and clear
The clarions rang; the Franks leapt from their palfreys,

And armed themselves with hauberks of fine steel,
With helms and golden-hilted swords, and spears
Astream with pennons white and red and blue;
Then mounted steeds of war, and spurred apace
Through the defiles, and each to other cried:
"If we but find Count Roland ere he die,
Beside him shall we give good blows." Alas!
To what avail? They will not come in time.

The hills are high and fearful, deep and dark
The valleys, where the rapid waters spring
Precipitously. The clarions ring through all
The mighty host, answering so the horn
Of Roland. And the great King rides in wrath,
And all his soldiers ride in wrath and sorrow.
Not one whose eyes fill not with tears, whose heart
Does not despair. Yet pray they unto God
That Roland may be saved until they come
To the red field. But what avails it now?
It is too late—they cannot come in time.

In anger rode the King, with his white beard
Tossed on his coat of mail. And all his Franks
Spurred on apace. Not one who does not pray
To come in time to Roland, where he fights
His last good fight. Alas, if Roland dies,
His men will all die with him. Sixty yet
Are fighting—sixty, good and true. No King
On the wide earth e'er captained better men.

the death of oliver

And Roland, meanwhile, standing from the stress
A moment, yielded him to grief, and wept.
Lo, where the mountains and the plains were strewed
With Frankish dead: "Great Paradise," he cried,
"Be granted unto you, and may your souls
Forever rest among its fragrant flowers.
No better liegemen ever were than you,
Who served me long and well. Nor may your King
Blame you in aught, for many a land is his
Through you. And this, alas, is your reward!
O France! dear country! as a desert land
Art thou laid waste on this ill omened day.
It is my fearful pride, Barons of France,
Has brought you face to face with death, and now
Mine arm is powerless to aid you—ay—
May He whose word is truth protect you now.
Oliver, friend, this day I die with you;
If not by hostile steel, of my own sorrow.
Enough of this! Join we the strife once more."

And so turned Roland to the field again.
He swung great Durendal, and woe to them
Who dared resist. They slaked his thirst for vengeance.
As runs the panting stag before the pack,
So fled the Saracens before his wrath.
And thus the Archbishop: "Roland, it is well.

He who bears arms, and sits on a good steed
Is thereby bounden to be brave and strong
Though facing fearful odds. Stands he not firm,
Nor fights with doubled strength, I should not give
Two farthings for him. Better he turned monk,
And found some peaceful cloister, where at least
His prayers might aid us." Roland, hearing, cried:
"Forward, good friends, and spare them not!" And so
They rushed once more where death awaited them.

He fights more desperately who knows full well
His foes are merciless. And so the Franks,
About to die, were terrible as lions.
Against them rode King Marsila, richly armed,
Sitting the steed of war he called his Hound.
Wrathfully spurring upon the Franks, he dealt
Relentless blows, shattering shields and spears,
Rending strong hauberks. Thus he smote and slew
Ivon and Ivor, ay, and old Girard
Of Roussillon. But lo, where Roland rode,
Crying: "May God bring woe upon you, wretch!
For slaying Christian knights in cause unjust
And impious. Here and now, before we part,
You will I teach the name of this my sword."
Then swung he Durendal, and with one blow
Drove the sharp steel through helm and head and frame
Of Marsila, till it found his wicked heart,
And his black soul went gibbering down to hell.
And his men cried: "Mahomet save us now!

O ye our gods, avenge us on this Charles,
Who into Spain hath brought such fearful fiends,
Who yield not, though they die." Then each to other
Shouted in terror: "Save himself who may!"
And with the word a hundred thousand fled
In utter rout, and none could rally them.

But what availed it? Though the Paynim King
Was dead, not so his uncle, he who ruled
The Carthaginian realm, far over seas,
And all the accursèd lands beyond. His men
Were inky black, big-nosed, wide-eared. They charged
Full fifty thousand strong, upon the Franks,
Rushing like angry demons of the world
Infernal, yelling the Paynim battle-cry.
And then spake Roland: "Now shall we achieve
Our martyrdom. Death is at hand. But first
Take we a price of blood for our sweet lives.
Once more, my lords, lay on with desperate strength,
Dispute ye well your lives, nay, deaths. Sweet France
Must not be shamed by us. When Charles shall come
To Ronceval, and find the field heaped high
With Paynims—ay, for every one of us
A score of them—he will be proud and glad."

When Roland saw the loathsome race draw near,
Blacker than pitch, nor showing any white
Unless of glistening teeth, he cried aloud:
"It is God's will we die. Would you obey

Your leader's last command, O Franks, die rudely!"
And Oliver then: "A curse on him who lags
And lives!" And so the Franks charged desperately.

Now that the Paynims saw the Franks were few
They were emboldened, swollen with great pride
Saying to one another: "Charles has lost
At last." And lo, the Carthaginian Caliph,
Spurring his steed, smote Oliver from behind—
A cowardly blow. The shining links were torn
Asunder, the merciless point of steel went through
The brave knight's body. Then the Paynim jeered:
"Think you the blow too rude? It was not kind
Of Charles the King to leave you here in Spain.
If he has wrought us ill, let him not boast
Thereof. For so, proud Frank, in slaying you
I balance—think you not?—the score of blood."

The Frankish knight was wounded unto death.
He swung good Halteclere, his burnished brand,
And smote the Paynim's pointed helm, o'erlaid
With flowers of yellow gold. The priceless gems
Flew from their mounts. Entered the steel, and clove
The Saracen's head down to the very teeth.
And Oliver laughed, and answered: "Wretched man,
I do not say Charles loses not somewhat
In this exchange of blood, but you are scarce
The gainer. Never will you, at home o'er seas,
To some fair woman boast of booty won

–67–

From Franks, nor yet of blows dealt unto me
Or any other man." And then he called
To Roland: "Help me, comrade, for I die."

The Frankish knight feels the sharp sting of death.
His heart is filled with thirst immeasurable
For vengeance. Where the fight is thickest, there
He rides, shivering shields and spears and helms.
Would you had seen him hew the Saracens,
Throwing them one upon other from their steeds
With well delivered blows, for so a knight
Should die—and all the while with ringing voice
Shouting the rallying cry of Charles his King.
And then he calls again: "Roland, your aid.
Stand you beside me yet once more. Alas,
Dear friend, the hour of parting is at hand."

And Roland looked upon his comrade's face—
Lo, it was colorless, drawn with fearful pain.
From his deep wound the blood leapt forth, and ran
In crimson streams over his coat of mail.
"God!" Roland cried. "I cannot bear this too!
Companion, your great fearlessness, unmatched
Among the Franks, has proved your own undoing.
Sweet France, how art thou spoiled of valiant men
This fearful day! How art thou fallen low!
Alas for Charles our King!" And with the word,
Yielding to grief, he swooned upon his steed.

Behold Count Roland, swooned upon his steed,
Behold his dear companion in the throes
Of death, whose eyes are darkened, who discerns
Nor friend nor foe. Lo, where the twain are borne
By coursing steeds together, and Oliver smites
His comrade's golden helm! Glances the blow
Entering not. And Roland came to sense,
And saw his lifelong comrade there, and said
In a low voice: "Friend, did you mean the blow?
I am your dear companion, whom you loved,
Who still loves you. You take me for a Paynim,
Else had you first defied me." And his friend
Made answer: "Now I hear your voice, and yet
I see you not. May God be not so blind!
Yes, I have struck you, friend. Forgive it me."
And Roland answered him with a great cry
Of love, and flung about him both his arms—
Alas, that two such friends must part forever!

The wounded knight feels the approach of death.
He cannot see or hear. So he dismounts
And kneels him down, raising on high his voice
Confesses him, clasping his hands implores
The gift of Paradise, and prays to God
For Charles his glorious King, and for sweet France,
But most of all for Roland, his companion.
His heart falters, his helmèd head sinks down
On his great breast, and slowly to the ground

He droops, and lies in death. His blessèd soul
Tarries no longer. Roland, when he saw,
Did cry aloud. A cry so terrible
Was never wrung from heart of mortal man.

When Roland saw his dear companion dead,
Lying face downward on the earth, his grief
Was uncontrolled. He called to him: "Sir friend,
Your valor merited a better meed
Than this! Day after day, year after year,
Have we been linked together in great love.
Life without you were deeper suffering
Than I could bear." And once again he swooned.
Held by his stirrups of gold, at the wild will
Of his mad steed, he traversed the red field.

the ARCHBISHOP

When Roland came to sense again, and looked
About him, all the Franks had fallen—all
Save the Archbishop. He afoot was fighting,
Thrown from his steed at last by Paynim spears.
But when he saw the Count, he hewed his way
To meet him, crying: "Nay, I yield me not!
A good knight yields him not in life." And so
With bright Almace, his sword of burnished steel,
In the thick press he struck a thousand blows.

And likewise Roland dealt good blows. But now
Fever consumed his strength, and in his head
Was fearful torment, where with the wild blast
His temples brake. Fain would he know if Charles
Were coming, and he raised his horn once more,
And feebly winded it. And the King heard,
And reined his steed, and said: "Hearken, my lords.
It fares not well with Roland—he is dying.
He would not wind so feebly, had he long
To live. If you would reach the field, give spur
To your good steeds. And let the clarions sound,
As many as there are in all the host."
And sixty thousand rang, and all the hills
Resounded, and the valleys answered them.
The Paynims heard, and laughed not, saying each
To other: "Hark! Now it is Charles who comes!"

The Paynims cried: "The King is coming. Hark!
The Frankish clarions near at hand are ringing.
If the King comes in time, and Roland lives,
This fearful war will start anew, and we
Shall lose forever the fair land of Spain."
Four hundred banded them together, ay,
Four hundred of the best, and all at once
On Roland charged—four hundred against one.

But Roland, when he saw them, wavered not,
Nor ever thought of yielding them the field
As long as life was in him. Through the flanks
Of his swift steed he drove his golden spurs,
And rode against the hostile swarm, and called
To Turpin: "Come, my friend, the Frankish horns
Are ringing clear, and Charles is near at hand."

So had he rushed on death, for he loved not
A coward, nor a cautious knight who stays
To count the foe. But when he saw that now
The Archbishop was on foot, he cried to him:
"You are unhorsed, and I for love of you
Draw rein, to stand with you. And we shall get
Or good or ill together, side by side.
Together shall we give as goodly blows
As we are given." And the Archbishop said:
"A curse on him who smites not rudely now!
And Charles is near at hand, to avenge our deaths."

And when the Paynims heard him, a great fear
Beset them, and they cried: "This day is fraught
With woe for us, ill fated. We have lost
Our captains and our fellows, and Charles comes
And with him his great host. For we can hear
The clarions of the fearful Franks; we hear
Their battle shout. And Roland is so strong
That he will never yield to mortal man.
Come, let us hurl our weapons all at once,
Then let him be." And so they threw their spears
And javelins and feathered shafts, and brake
And rent his shield, and yet pierced not his body,
But slew his faithful steed. And then they fled,
And let him be—on foot, but still in life.

In fear and impotent rage the Paynims fled
From Ronceval, and Roland followed not,
For his good steed was dead. He turned to help
The Archbishop Turpin, from his head unlaced
The golden helm, stripped off his shining hauberk,
Cut his white tunic into bands, and so
Bound his deep wounds. And then he lifted him
In both his arms, and carried him where grew
The soft green grass, and gently spake: "Good friend,
Our comrades, whom we held so dear, are dead.
We must not in this hour forget them—nay,
I go to seek them out, and bring them here,
For you to bless." And Turpin answered: "Go!
This field is yours, thanks be to God, and mine."

And Roland, all alone, traversed the field
Of strife, searching the vales and the high hills.
And so he found, lying where they had fought,
Gerin and Gerier, Anselm called the Proud,
Berengier, and Girard of Roussillon,
Ivon and Ivor, Otto, and at last
The Dukes of Gascony and Burgundy;
And one by one he carried them where knelt
The good Archbishop, and gently laid them down
Before him. Turpin wept, and raised his hand,
And blessed them, saying: "Sirs, an evil fate
Has come upon you. God receive your souls
Among the flowers of heaven, and there, my friends,
If He is willing, shall I come this day
To greet you, for I die. Mine hour is come.
I shall not look again on the great King."

But Roland turned once more to search the field,
And found his comrade, Oliver. Him he raised,
And gently carried where the Archbishop knelt,
And laid him on his shield beside his friends.
And the Archbishop blessed him, marking him
With the true Cross, and Roland wept, and said:
"Oliver, comrade, son of the great Duke
Of Genoa, none like you could meet the shock
Of lance, or shatter shield of Saracen,
Or conquer and confound the arrogant. None
Like you could counsel valiant men. Than you
There was no better knight in all the world."

And Roland, when he saw the Peers of France
Lying in death, and with them his dear friend,
Whom he had loved so long, was overcome
By his great sorrow. His tears broke forth anew,
And fearful pallor overspread his face,
And from his suffering he swooned, and fell
Upon the earth. And Turpin cried: "Alas!
Must he die too? the noblest of them all!"

And when he saw him swoon, his grief was more
Than he could bear. But he put forth his hand
And took the horn from Roland's side, for down
Through Ronceval there ran a limpid stream,
And so he thought to help his friend. In pain,
With little, tottering steps, he turned him there,
But could not reach the goal, so weak was he
For loss of blood. A furlong did he grope—
Then his heart failed him utterly, and he fell
Upon the grass, and knew that death was near.

But Roland, meanwhile, coming from his swoon,
And standing on his feet, for all his pain,
Looked up and down the battlefield. And there
On the green grass, beyond his comrades all,
Lay the Archbishop—he whom God had made
His representative in France. With hands
Upraised and joined, confessing all his sins,
Prayed he to God that heaven be granted him.
Turpin is dead, the warrior of great Charles.

With blows well given no less than goodly words,
Ever was he a champion of the Faith
Against the Paynims. May God receive his soul!

And when Count Roland saw him lying there
In death, the red blood flowing free from wounds
Innumerable, he crossed his fair, white hands
Upon his silent heart, and wept, and said:
"O noble comrade, you do I commend
To God in heaven, for never mortal man
Served him more faithfully, nor since the time
Of the apostles has a better man
Upheld the Faith and saved the perishing.
May your great soul be glad, and may the gates
Of glorious heaven be opened wide for you."

the death of Roland

Roland, for death was imminent—from his wounds
A crimson flood was flowing—prayed to God
For the great Peers, and prayed for his own soul
To Gabriel the Archangel. Then he took
His horn in his left hand, and in his right
His trusted sword, lest any man reproach
His fair name afterward, and so went forth
Through a green field toward Paynim Spain, as far
As arrow flies from bow, and climbed a hill
Where two great trees flung heavenward their arms,
And covered with their shadows four hewn blocks
Of marble. There, on the soft grass, he fell
Headlong, and swooned, and death was near at hand.

The hills were high, and high upsprang the trees
Over the four white stones, and the green grass.
A Paynim, feigning death, had smeared his face
And all his frame with blood, and thrown him down
On a great heap of dead men. Now he rose
To his full height, a stalwart man and strong,
And ran to Roland, laying craven hand
Upon him. And he cried aloud: "Now yields
The nephew of great Charles; this sword shall I
Take home to Araby!" So he spake, and touched
The golden hilt, and Roland came to sense.

When Roland felt that a strange hand had grasped
His Durendal, he opened his dim eyes,
And cried: "Hold! You are not a friend, methinks."
And seized the horn beside him, and did smite
So fearfully upon the Paynim's helm,
He crushed both helm and head, and threw him down
A lifeless clod. And then he said: "You coward!
How were you ever bold enough, for right
Or wrong, to lay on me your arrogant hands?
Unhappy wretch! for all who hear of this
Shall deem you madman—but mine ivory horn
Is shattered, and the golden rim is broken."

And Roland, though his eyes were dimmed, though death
Was near at hand, gathered his strength once more,
And stood upon his feet. Before him lay
A marble stone. In pain and fearful wrath
He swung bright Durendal, and smote upon
The unyielding rock. The quivering steel rang loud,
But broke not, nor was splintered, and he cried:
"Saint Mary, aid me! Durendal my sword,
In evil hour they forged you. I must you
Forsake, and cherish you no more—with whom
So many battles have I fought, and won
So many lands, which he of the white beard
Now holds. God give that none possess you now
Save that he know not cowardice. Good sword,
A valiant knight and true has wielded you.
A better man is not—mayhap—in France."

And Roland smote the marble stone. The steel
Rang loud, but splintered not. And when he knew
He could not break the tempered blade, he cried:
"O Durendal, how white you are, and how
You gleam, aflame in the bright sun! The King—
They say—was holding court in Morianne,
And lo, an herald came from God, and bade
That you be given to one of his great captains—
Then girt he all your brightness upon me.
With you I conquered Brittany for the King,
Normandy, Aquitania, Lombardy,
And all Roumania. And with you I won
Bavaria and great Flanders, Burgundy,
Poland and far Stamboul, which swore to serve
My master always, and his will is law
Among the fair-haired Saxons. And with you
I conquered for him Scotland and fierce Wales,
And Ireland, and he holds for his domain
All England too. With you I overcame
All the broad lands that Charles of the white beard
Now holds. But I grieve for you, my Durendal,
Thinking that you shall stay henceforth in Spain—
With Saracens! O God, let not this be!"

And Roland smote the stone, and hewed away
A fragment. The good steel rang loud and clear,
Yet shattered not nor splintered, but upsprang
Toward heaven, and Roland knew it would not break
For all his desperate strength. And tenderly then

He spake to it: "O Durendal, how fair
You are, and holy, for your pommel hides
Good store of relics—ay, a tooth of Peter,
A vial of Basil's martyred blood, and hair
Of good Saint Dennis, and the blessèd hem
Of Mary's garment. He who wields you now
Must be a Christian. And may God forfend
That Saracens possess you, or a man
Who ever falters. O sweet Durendal,
How many lands has Roland won with you,
Now held by Charles the Great, whose beard is white
As driven snow, ruler of all the Franks."

And then he knew that death was taking hold
Of his great frame, creeping from head to heart.
Under a lofty pine, on the green grass
He cast him down, laying his horn and sword
Beneath him, turning his face where fled
The affrighted Paynims, that the King might know
He died a conqueror still, and lifted voice
To heaven, confessing him to his liege lord,
Tendering him the glove of his right hand.

Ay—Roland knew that death was near. He lay
On a high hill, looking toward Paynim Spain,
And beat his breast, crying: "Forgive, O God,
The wrongs that I have wrought Thee, since the day
When I was born unto this day when here
I am fordone." He raised his iron glove

To the blue sky, and so the angels came
On wings of gold to take his soul to God.

    Under a lofty pine he lay, and turned
Toward Spain, and called to memory many things—
The lands that he had conquered, and sweet France,
His kindred, and Great Charles, who cherished him
As his own son. And yet, for all his grief,
Remembered how a knight should pray, and said:
"Father whose word is truth, who from the grave
Didst ransom Lazarus, and from ravening lions
Didst rescue Daniel, rescue now my soul
From suffering for the sins which I have sinned
All my life long." And so upon his arm
His head sank slowly down. With joinèd hands,
Praying, he died. And as he died there came
On golden wings a spirit, and beside
Saint Michael of the Peril of the Deep,
And the Archangel Gabriel, and these three
Carried his soul to heaven, and to God.

the punishment of the paynims

Roland is dead. In heaven his great soul rests
With God his Father. And now the King had come
To Ronceval, and found nor road nor path,
Nor bit of field an ell or foot in width,
Where lay not stretched in death a Saracen
Or Frank. And the King called in a loud voice:
"Where are you, Roland? Where the Archbishop? Ay,
And Oliver, your friend? What have you done
With Gerin and bold Gerier, and the Dukes
Of Gascony and fruitful Burgundy?
With Ivon and with Ivor, whom I loved?
Where are Berengier, Anselm called the Proud,
Otto, and old Girard of Roussillon?
Where are the Peers of France, whom I did leave
With you in Spain?" But what availed his words?
For none could answer them. And then he cried:
"Why was I not with Roland when the fight
Was on?" and wept, and tore his beard. The Franks
Wept with him, and were seized by fearful faintness.
The oldest of them all, for all the years
Of his long life, had never known such grief.

There was no man in all the Frankish host
Who wept not bitterly, mourning son or brother
Or nephew, mourning friends and their liege lords—
Ay, many a strong, rude warrior, overcome

By a strange faintness, fell to earth, and swooned.
But Naimon first remembered there was work
For all to do, and spake to Charles, and said:
"Look yonder, two good leagues ahead—in shrouds
Of swirling dust the Spanish highroads lie.
There flee the Paynim hosts. To horse, O King!
Avenge us now." And Charles made answer, saying:
"Unless they be too far away. O God!
Teach me to take just vengeance—I have lost
The flower of France." And then he called four knights,
Four whom he trusted well, and bade them guard
The battlefield of Ronceval, and let
The dead men lie, untouched by ravening beasts
Of earth or air, untouched by impious hand
Of any mortal man, until God willed
That he should come again to the sad field.
And they made answer: "Sire, it shall be done."
And with them stayed a thousand of their men.

And Charles bade sound the trumpets, and rode on
With the great host. As one man followed they
The fleeing Paynims, while the evening sun
Sank in the west. And when the King saw darkness
Coming, he reined his steed, and set his foot
On the soft grass, and knelt, and prayed to God
That the red sun might stay its course, and day
Not die too soon. And lo! an angel came
From heaven, who cried to Charles: "Ride on! for day
Shall fail you not. Ay, you have lost the flower

Of France, and God himself enjoins you now
To vengeance." So he spake, and then did Charles,
With lightened heart, leap to his steed again.

Through God's great love for Charles a wondrous thing
Was wrought, for the red sun stood still
While Paynims fled, and Franks pursued, and so
They caught them in the valley that men call
The Vale of Darkness. Then relentlessly
They urged their quarry on; and many of them
They slew, and drove the rest from the highroad
Into the Ebro's waters, deep and swift
And fearful. Barge was there not, nor skiff, nor boat
Of any kind. They called upon their god
Of stone, and so leapt in—he helped them not,
For some, heavy with armor, sank at once.
And some were whirled amid yet blacker waves.
They who fared best drank deep enough, and all
Were miserably drowned. And the Franks cried:
"This is the price you pay for Roland's death!"

And when they told the King that none was left
In life, for all had been or slain or drowned,
He set his foot to earth, and knelt him down,
And thanked his God. And when he rose again,
The lingering sun had set. And the King said:
"Now may we rest, but turn we not this night
To Ronceval. The way is hard and long,
And our good steeds are wearied. From their backs

Unstrap the saddles, from their heads unloose
The bridles, and let them graze in the wide fields
At will"—and gladly was his word obeyed.

And so the great King rested, and his host.
In that still vale, where no man save themselves
Remained, they set their feet on earth, and slipped
The saddles from their steeds, and from their heads
The golden bridles, and gave them the wide fields
For manger. Then, outworn at last, they took
No thought of else, and slept in all their armor,
Under the stars. That night no guard was set.

the Lament of the King

At the first touch of dawn, the King awoke,
And the Archangel Gabriel, sent by God
To guard him sleeping, signed him with the cross.
And he arose, and stripped him of his hauberk,
And all the host laid off their arms, and leapt
On their swift steeds, and rode through narrow path
And broad highway to Ronceval, where died
Roland and all his men, in fearful fight.

And when the King had come to Ronceval,
And rode among the dead, he wept, and said
To his chief men: "My lords, rein in your steeds,
For I would fain precede you. Let me find
My nephew Roland ere you follow. Ay—
Years ago, in my vaulted hall at Aix,
Methinks it was a Christmastide—my knights
Were vaunting them of prowess and high deeds
Upon the field of battle, and Roland said
That he should never die in a strange land
Save at the head of all his men, with face
Turned to the foe, and victory in his heart."
He spake, and went before the rest, the space
One throws a spear, and climbed to a high hill.

And when he rode among the dead, he found
The fair, white flowers all crimson with the blood

Of his brave men, and kept not back his tears.
And so he came where sprang two lofty trees
Toward heaven, and saw, on the three stones, the marks
Of Roland's sword, and saw his nephew lying
On the green grass beyond. And Charles cried out
In his great sorrow, and leapt to earth, and ran
And took him in his arms. Then lost all sense,
And fell to earth, so fearful was his grief.

But when at last he came from out his swoon,
Old Naimon and three knights, with gentle hands
Lifted him up, and laid him with his back
Against a pine tree. And he looked and saw
His nephew lying dead, and thus he spake:
"Roland, dear friend, may God be merciful
To your great soul. Your equal never lived
For the first blows of battle, or the last.
I lose in you the half of all my fame."
And then he swooned again, so deep his grief.

And when he came to sense, four of his knights
Upheld him in their arms. And the King looked,
And saw his nephew lying stretched in death,
Handsome for all his pallor, and the darkness
Of his eyes. And he said to him again:
"Roland, true friend, may God receive your soul
Among the flowers of heaven. O wretched me!
Who brought you into Spain, and for mine own
Undoing. All my life is darkened, ay,

The sun of my great power and pride is setting.
None such as you shall fight for me again,
For there is none—methinks—of all the Franks,
Of mine own kindred even, who is brave
Like you." He spake, and tore with frenzied hands
His hair, and all his men were filled with sorrow,
And there was none who wept not bitterly.

"Roland, my truest friend, when I shall come
Once more to France, and once again shall sit
Upon my golden throne, at home in Laon,
From many lands will come my liegemen, saying:
'Where is great Roland? What have you done with him?'
And I shall say that he is dead in Spain.
In grief immeasurable shall I possess
The darkened realm of France. Ay—every day
Shall see my tears, and hear my cries of grief.

"Friend! hero! fairest of the fair young men
Of France! When I shall come to Aix once more,
And be within my chapel, men will ask
For you. And I shall answer them, and say:
'Dead is my nephew, dead! Who won for me
So many widespread lands.' And then, alas,
The Saxons will rise up against me—ay—
And all the hostile tribes of Hungary
And wild Bulgaria, and the barbarous men
Of Afric and the lands that lie beyond.

Then will increase my travail, and my toil
Will be too great, for who shall lead my host
Against such hordes, when he is dead in Spain
Who used to captain us? Unhappy France,
For thou art left forlorn this fearful day!
And I would fain not live." He tore his beard,
And with both hands his hair, white as the snow
New fallen, and all his soldiers wept for him.

"Friend! God be merciful, and give your soul
Great Paradise. The spear that pierced your heart
Has pierced the heart of France. I would fain die
For loss of you, and for the loss of all
Who fought and died for me in Ronceval.
O God, as Thou hast taken unto Thee
Their blessèd souls, so take Thou mine this day,
And let my body here be laid in earth,
In the same grave with theirs." He spake, and tore
His beard, and all the Franks wept for their King.

And then spake Naimon: "Bid us search the field
And find our friends who fought and died for us.
That we may pray for them, and bury them."

He raised his hand. The horns of all the host
Rang loud. The Franks, dismounting, sought their friends
And brought them to the King, and tonsured priests
Absolved and signed them with the cross of God,

And burned sweet myrrh and spices. So they laid
Their comrades in one grave, and left them there
In Spain. Alas! there was no other way.

But the King bade them tenderly upraise
The three most noble of the martyred host
Of France—Roland, and Oliver, his friend,
And the Archbishop. And they took the hearts
From out their bodies, and in precious silk
Enveloped them, and laid them in a shrine
Of purest marble, and the bodies wrapped
In skins of the red deer, anointing them
With wine and spices. Then did loving hands
Lift them on three black wains, and covered them
With a white pall of Alexandrine silk,
And carried them upon the toilsome march
Over the high and strait defiles. And so
In sorrow came they back to France once more.
And in the church of Blaye did Charles the King
Bury Count Roland and his gentle friend
And the Archbishop. In three marble tombs
He laid them, and commended them to God.
And there they lie in peace unto this day.

ALDA

King Charles turned him from Spain, and came to Aix,
The richest town of France, and sat again
In his great hall, and lo! before him stood
Alda, fairest of women. Thus she spake:
"Where is Count Roland, he who swore to me
To take me for his bride?" And Charles the King
Was sad, and wept, and tore his snow-white beard.
"Sister, sweet friend, Roland has not come back
From Spain. But I shall give you in his stead
Mine eldest son, who after me shall hold
My kingdom; fairer barter know I not."
But she: "These words are as strange tongue to me.
May God forfend, and may His saints forfend
That I should live without him!" So she swooned,
And fell at the King's feet, and straight was dead.
May God in heaven have mercy on her soul!

Alda, fairest of Frankish girls, is dead.
And when the King, thinking she had but swooned,
In tears and sad compassion took her hands,
Upraising her from earth, her head fell back
Upon her shoulders. Then he knew that death
Was come. He called four ladies of his court,
And silently they bore her to a church
Where nuns kept tearful vigil till the dawn;
Then was she gently laid in holy ground,
Beside the highest altar. In her name
Charles the great King enriched the church tenfold.

the punishment of ganelon

And when the King returned from Ronceval,
In iron chains lay Ganelon. Him they brought
To the great square, and tied him to a post
With leathern thongs, and beat him fearfully
With staves and knotted ropes—and he deserved
No else. But judgment yet awaited him.

And Charles, so it is written in the Book
Of Frankish Kings, summoned from many lands
His men, and gathered them in his own church.
It was a day of festival, some say
Of blessèd Saint Sylvester, and there and then
Was Ganelon judged before the throne of Charles.

"My lords," said Charles the King, "what punishment
Is meet for Ganelon, who in Paynim Spain
Gave death to twenty thousand men of mine
On Ronceval's red field? And he betrayed
For gold my nephew, whom no mortal man
Shall see again, and Oliver his friend,
The brave and courteous, and the twelve great Peers
Of France." And Ganelon answered, saying: "Ay,
But Roland sent me wilfully to death
In Saragossa. Him I slew, as me
He would have slain. But treason was it not."
And the Franks said: "Sit we in judgment now."

Before his sovereign Ganelon strode, and stood,
A handsome man, in the strong flush of life;
Had he been good and true, you would have said
He was the best of all the Frankish knights.
And he, undaunted, looking on the men
Chosen to judge his cause, and on his kindred—
For thirty stood beside him—cried aloud:
"For God's sweet love, hearken! my lords! The King
Speaks truth, saying that I was in the host
That conquered Spain, and him I served in faith
And love. But Roland hated me, and so
Adjudged me unto suffering and death.
Roland it was who sent me to the King
Of Paynim Spain, and I living returned
Through mine own cunning. True it is I took
A swift and fearful vengeance, not alone
On Roland, but on Oliver his friend,
And all their comrades—lawful vengeance though,
For had I not defied them? Charles the King
Heard me, and heard me all his soldiers. Thus
I paid them all—but treason was it not."
And the Franks said: "You shall have judgment now."

And Ganelon, hearing, straightway turned him where
His thirty kinsmen stood, and in their midst
He whom they all acknowledged as their lord,
Pinabel, Castellan of Sorence, renowned
For his fair speech, yet more for fighting well
Upon the field of battle. To him spake

Ganelon, saying: "Friend, I trust in you.
Save me this day from calumny and death."
And he: "Fear not. If any mortal man
Adjudge thee to be hanged, shall this my sword
Give him the lie, when or wherever the King
Shall bid us fight till death." And Ganelon then,
Glad with new courage, knelt before his friend.

So to their council turned the chosen Franks
And all the judges, some from Normandy
And bright Auvergne, and some from Saxon lands
And far Bavaria—ay, and many others.
But all because of Pinabel were afraid,
Timidly saying each to other: "Come,
Let be this thing. Implore we the great King
To pardon Ganelon, who shall swear an oath
To serve him from this day in love and faith.
Roland is dead—nor silver nor red gold
Can bring him back. And surely he is mad
Who champions dead men." Thus the cowards spake.

And so they came to the great King of France,
And knelt before his throne, and him implored
To pardon whom he hated, if he swore
To serve him from that day in love and faith.
"Let him not die. It is too late. His death
Will not bring back the dead, when all the gold
Of all the world is powerless." But the King
Made wrathful answer: "Cowards are you all!"

And the King's face was darkened, when he saw
That all were faithless. Crying out as one
Pierced to the heart, he cursed them all. And lo,
There leapt before his throne a valiant knight,
Count Thierry, younger brother of Duke Geoffrey,
Black-haired, and bronzed by Spanish suns, in build
Slender and supple, nor tall nor overshort.
And thus he spake to the great King: "O Charles,
Despair not thus, for there is one at least
To serve you, one who has not will alone
But lawful right to serve you, for I spring
From noble stock. Whatever wrong was done
By Roland, he fought for you, and that alone
Gave him the right to live. He who betrayed
The King's best soldier, betrayed the King as well.
And I adjudge him to be hanged, and thrown
His worthless corpse to dogs and ravening beasts
Of prey. Let him die a traitor's death! God's wounds!
If there be any who shall say me nay,
With this my girded sword shall I not fail
To uphold my judgment." And the listening Franks
Applauded, crying: "You have spoken well."

Pinabel stood before the King—a knight
Swifter of foot than any steed of war,
And tall and strong and brave, and whom he smote
Tarried not long among his fellow men.
And to the King he said: "Sire, it is yours

To be obeyed. Command there be an end
Of idle clamor. Here I give the lie
To this Count Thierry, and will fight with him."
Into the King's right hand he put his glove
Of tawny deerskin, who made answer, "Ay,
But you must give good hostages," and straight
His kinsmen, thirty of them, pledged themselves.
And likewise did the King give hostages,
And bade his soldiers guard them, till the fight
Was ended, and God had shown the truth to all.

And when Count Thierry likewise laid his glove
In the King's hand, they brought to a wide field
Benches of wood, where sat them down the twain,
Until the chosen judges, at their head
Ogier of Denmark, bade them gird themselves.
And then the brave knights called for steeds and arms.

But ere they joined in mortal strife, confessed
Their carnal sins, and holy priests absolved
And signed them with the cross, and mass was sung,
And blessèd bread and wine were tasted—ay,
The twain made gifts to the great church of Aix.
And then they stood before the King, and fixed
Their spurs upon their feet, and blithely donned
Their coats of mail, burnished and strong and light,
And girt their swords, and hung their quartered shields
About their shoulders, and took their spears, and mounted.
And all the Franks were sad, remembering

Their captain, Roland, fearing for his fame,
For God alone knows what the end shall be.

Below the town a green field lay, and there
They fought together. First, they loosed their reins,
Drove deep their spurs, and rode each upon other,
And shattered each the other's shield, and rent
His linkèd hauberk, and cut his saddle girth.
The leathern saddles turned, and threw the riders
Headlong—and all who saw cried out in fear.

Both knights were thrown to earth, but in a flash
Sprang to their feet, and let their chargers be,
And rushed each on the other with drawn swords,
And each the other's helmet smote, with blows
That well-nigh shattered them. And all the Franks
Cried out in fear; and the King knelt, and prayed.

And while the swords were clashing, Pinabel cried:
"Yield! Yield! Count Thierry, and I swear an oath
To be your faithful liegeman all my life,
Giving you of my worldly goods as much
As you desire; and then shall you accord
Ganelon and the King." But he made answer,
"Nay, I shall never yield me while I live.
This day must God uphold or you or me!"

And while the swords rang loud, Count Thierry cried:
"Sir, you are famed among the Franks, for you

Are tall and strong as some great towering crag,
And none would call you coward. Enough! Let be
This fight, and I shall make your peace with Charles
Then shall the traitor have such punishment
As shall be whispered fearfully while men
Live upon earth." But Pinabel answered him:
"May God forfend that ever I be false
To my own kindred. Nay, far better die
Than hear through all my life the scornful words
Of them who trusted me." And with their swords
They ever smote, and from the helms of steel,
Covered with gems and gold, the bright sparks flew
Heavenward. None may part them now, for death,
Grim death alone, can end this fearful strife.

And then with all his strength did Pinabel
Heave his great sword, and smote the other's helm,
And from the fire thereof the grass was kindled.
Down crashed the trenchant blade, cleaving the helm
Asunder. The sharp steel drew crimson blood
From Thierry's cheek, and ever tearing down
Rent the bright hauberk on his breast. But God,
In His great mercy, kept the knight from death.

But when Count Thierry felt the biting steel
Upon his face, and saw his own red blood
On the green grass about him, sudden rage
Gave him new strength, and with a fearful cry
He swung his heavy sword on high and down

Upon his rival's helmet. The keen blade
Cut through, and found the flesh and bone beneath—
No mortal man could feel that blow, and live.
And so the fight was ended, and the Franks
Cried with one voice: "It is the will of God!
Thus has He shown the right. Let Ganelon
Be hanged, and with him all his hostages."

Then to the victor came the King, with arms
Outstretched, and followed by his best loved knights,
Naimon, and Ogier, he of Denmark—ay,
And many others. And the King embraced
His champion, with the hem of his great cloak
Wiping the crimson blood from the deep gash
Upon his cheek. Then gently they disarmed him,
And on a mule of Araby he rode
Back to the city, honored by them all.
But when they came to Aix, and in the square
Set foot to earth, the traitor Ganelon
Was brought to judgment, and his hostages.

And Charles gathered his counsellors, and said:
"What shall I do with those who pledged their lives
For love of Ganelon, those who cast their lot
With Pinabel?" And they, by Frankish law,
Adjudged them all to death. And Charles the King
Bade hang them all on one accursèd tree,
And swore by his white beard, if one escaped,
The executioner should pay for him

With his own life. Whereto the hangman answered
With a grim laugh, and "Never fear, my lord,"
And bade a hundred of his men drag off
The thirty hostages. And so they died,
Paying the price of treachery, for it brings
Black death to others, not to self alone.

But ere the judges turned them home—for some
Had come to Aix from Brittany, and some
From Normandy, or far Bavaria—ay,
From many a distant country—they adjudged
A fearful death to Ganelon, for they bade
That he be strongly fettered hand and foot
To four swift steeds, and then a furious mob
Drove them with sharpened sticks through a wide field
His mortal frame was rent apart, his limbs
Torn from his wretched body, and his blood
Crimsoned the grass. So perished Ganelon—ay,
If any man betray a fellow man,
It is not right that he should boast thereof.